The Complete Book of
SURFING

The
Complete Book
of SURFING

by Peter L. Dixon

Illustrated with Photographs,
Drawings and Maps

Coward-McCann, Inc.
New York

Contents

Introduction

THERE is really no one way to express the feeling that a good ride on a big fast-moving wave brings to surfers. Some surfers get *stoked*, others are exhilarated, a few are blasted, but most feel deeply satisfied when the wave was perfect and the ride long. The experience of surfing has drawn thousands to the waves. New surfers are beginning a sport that started many hundreds of years ago in Polynesia, and after a period of quiet has been born again. Surfing is now international and surfers challenge the sea from Australia to Atlantic City, from Hawaii to Peru, and from South Africa to Malibu.

Why the sudden explosive interest in surfing? What draws people into the cold water, to the pounding waves, to the hazards of cuts on sharp coral and collisions with other surfers? Why do surfers fly and drive and sail thousands of miles to be blasted off their board by a wave? Why have thousands and thousands all over the world bought or built boards? And finally what is there about surfing that captures the imagination and satisfies some fulfillment of the mind and body?

There are several qualities to surfing that may provide some answers. Surfing is the most individualistic of all sports. Alone on a board, speeding over a wave at fifteen or twenty miles an hour, the surfer experiences an ecstatic communication with natural forces, a delicious isolation, and total freedom from the anxieties and mundane cares of the workaday world.

Surfing is also a challenge requiring intense concentration. The total range of senses is engaged in keeping the body in balance and the wave from dominating the rider. This is particularly true in big surf. On smaller, well-formed waves there is time to look around, wave to a friend and plan ahead. But the surfer who lets his attention lag will lose to the wave. Waves are living, moving things and, like people, no two waves are alike. This infinite variety gives surfing color, excitement, action. Yet surfing is uncomplicated. In the frightfully complex world of modern technology nothing is quite as refreshingly simple as a functional surfboard and waves, sun, and sky.

Surfers as a rule are not worriers. I've never experienced a worry sitting on a board waiting for a wave and I've never known a surfer who was troubled out on the water. This escape from the ordinary is certainly a part of surfing, as is the feeling of being unique. Many have observed that younger surfers start the sport because of the status it gives them. But whatever the motivation, the surfer must still face the sea and the waves.

Some of the famous Hawaiian big-surf riders feel compelled to *challenge* the surf; they see this flirtation with accident and death as a striving for power over nature. One famous big-waver claims that riding mountain-size waves gives him a feeling of immortality. Some are attracted by the grinding cameras of surf film producers and the admiring throng on the beach.

The popularity of surfing has created problems. The demand for surfing areas has resulted in crowded waves at some beaches, and the danger from collision is ever present. Learning to surf *well* adds to the safety and enjoyment of the sport. The beginner needs to practice, and practice hard if he wants to become expert. There are really no short cuts for actual experience on a board, but some of the knowledge gained by others can be passed on to the new surfer. This book was written to help smooth the way and provide a better understanding of what happens when man and wave meet.

Chapter 1

THE HISTORY OF SURFING

THE sport of surfing originated early in man's history, somewhere in the West Pacific, probably in the area called Oceania. The people who learned to capture the energy of the surf and use it for their pleasure were Polynesians. Their home was most likely the islands of Tahiti and Bora Bora. A group of these Polynesians left their home islands sometime between A.D. 800 and 1100 and migrated eastward. Their long overwater migration took them to the Hawaiian Islands. Probably stowed in the hulls of their giant catamaran canoes were the original prototypes of today's modern surfboard. The Polynesians found Hawaii a garden island and they flourished there. Along with the bountiful land was the surf needed to ride their boards, and over the years these early settlers of Hawaii enjoyed the surf and gave it ritual and meaning that affected the lives of both kings and commoners.

On a February day in 1778 their tropical island was spied by a lookout atop the mast of a British ship under the command of Captain Cook. As the great seaman and explorer sailed into Hawaii his astonished crew spotted some men who appeared to be flying over the water. What they saw were Hawaiian nobility riding waves on their huge wiliwili-wood surfboards. These early Hawaiians were an impressive people and their princes were tall and vigorous. To an Eng-

11

The long board is the Olo, used by early Hawaiian royalty; the shorter ones were for ordinary folk.

Ron Church

lish seaman of the eighteenth century, the six-and-a-half-foot Hawaiian standing erect and riding a huge wave must have been a wonderous sight.

The early boards were called olos, and the wiliwili wood from which they were made was almost as light as balsa. The olos were reserved for royalty while the shorter and heavier boards (koas) were used by the commoners. The early Hawaiians treated their boards with care and respect. After surfing the boards were dried, rubbed down with oil, and carefully put away. Today, at the Bishop Museum in Honolulu, a few of the early Hawaiian surfboards are on display. These prototypes of today's plastic and fiberglass boards are long and narrow, about twenty inches wide and five to six inches thick. The long boards of the royalty often weighed over a hundred pounds. One of the boards on permanent display in the museum is over sixteen feet long. Hawaiian history tells of surfing beaches reserved for the exclusive use of royalty, forbidden to commoners under penalty of death.

Captain Cook's *A Voyage to the Pacific Ocean*, Vol. III, contains the first recorded account of early Hawaiian surfing:

> Whenever, from stormy weather, or any extraordinary swell at sea, the impetuosity of the surf is increased to its utmost height, they choose that time for this amusement which is performed in the following manner: twenty or thirty of the natives, taking each a long narrow board, rounded at the ends, set out together from shore. The first wave they meet, they plunge under, and suffering to roll over them, rise again beyond it, and make the best of their way by swimming, out to sea. The second wave is encountered in the same manner with the first; the great difficulty consisting in seizing the proper moment of diving under it, which, if missed, the person is caught by the surf, and driven back again with great violence; and all his dexterity is then required to prevent himself from being dashed against the rocks. As soon as they have gained, by these repeated efforts, the smooth water beyond the surf, they lay themselves at length on their boards, and prepare for their return. As the surf consists of a number of waves, of which every third is remarked to be always larger than the others, and to flow higher on the shore, the rest breaking in the immediate space, their first object is to place themselves on the summit of the largest surge, by which they are driven along with amazing rapidity toward the shore." Captain Cook concludes by saying, "The boldness and address, with which we saw them perform these difficult and dangerous maneuvers, was altogether astonishing, and is scarce to be credited.

Cook's report also mentions canoe surfing and women surfers. Surfing went along smoothly for the next fifty-seven years, the Hawaiians begetting and playing and feasting and surfing in their happy ways, until the arrival of the Calvinist missionaries from Boston in 1821. The impact of missionary zeal upon native culture brought about the end of most surfing in Hawaii for almost a hundred years. Along with muumuus to cover their bodies, guilt and sin to cloud their souls, the people from civilization brought plague and disease to reduce the population. The missionaries banned the hula and the music and the sports that kept the islanders healthy. There was a revival of surfing under the rule of King Kalakaua, but his reign was brief, and surfing took second place to sugar plantations and the annexation of Hawaii by the United States.

In the early years of the twentieth century, when hotels, tourism and commerce were developing in and around Waikiki Beach, the first surf clubs started and the sport began to grow in popularity again. Largely responsible for surfing's rebirth was one of the most famous modern Hawaiians, Duke Kahanamoku. The Duke went to the 1912 and 1920 Olympic Games and brought back a gold medal in the 100-meter free-style swim. The pride in swimming and watermanship which the Duke revised in the islands, and his work in forming surfing clubs, helped shape modern surfing.

The Pacific Electric Railroad played an important role in bringing surfing to California. Shortly before World War I the Pacific Electric began shoving their tracks throughout Southern California. This was in the days of the great land boom (still going strong), and the local railroads put in tracks before the population moved in. Ticket sales were somewhat slow on the P&E's beach route and the company decided a sales promotion campaign was needed. P&E hired George Freeth to put on surfing exhibitions at Redondo Beach. George was an Irish-Hawaiian, and an extraordinarily talented swimmer and surfer. His surfboard demonstrations up and down the coast drew thousands of spectators and gave surfing its start in California.

Duke Kahanamoku sailed for California shortly after this and gave additional demonstrations which further strengthened interest in surfing. The Duke also visited Australia in 1915 and his surfing exploits at Freshwater Beach, Sydney, started the still growing surfing boom down under. During the 1920's, interest in surfing continued to grow in California and Hawaii. In the late 1920's, Tom Blake designed and built a hollow surfboard that was quite fast and paddled easily. With his new design, Blake proceeded to win most of the surfing and paddling events he entered. The first Blake boards were hundred-pounders but further design refinement brought the weight down to a more manageable sixty pounds. His boards were long and narrow—more like paddleboards than surfboards. The Blake hollow board and the solid pine and redwood boards set the pattern in the years prior to World War II.

Surfers grew tired of hauling around the heavy planks and there was a continual search to find lighter, more easily paddled boards. Several variations of the solid board were tried; some had balsa centers and others were part hollow. The great all-time California surfer and waterman Pete Peterson built a pair of very light all-balsawood boards in the 1930's, but the wood was soft and fragile and the varnish coating cracked easily. The balsa then became waterlogged and heavy, and eventually rotted. The all-balsa idea was basically sound and with the discovery of fiberglass cloth and the plastic resins to laminate the glass to wood, the modern surfboard was born. Fiberglass covered balsa boards immediately caught on and soon were produced commercially by Joe Quigg, Mat Kivlin, Dale Velzy, and Bob Simmons. Simmons, with his engineering background, developed a foam-filled board after World War II that pioneered today's types. The author once owned one of these early Simmons boards. It was rather remarkable. The foam core was sandwiched between two layers of marine plywood, and the board was then covered with glass cloth.

The light balsa boards had many advantages. They could be carried by an average man or woman, they paddled easily and were very buoyant. The increased buoyancy resulted in smaller boards being built, and smaller boards resulted in more maneuverability and made the present style of modern surfing possible. Surfing stunts and styles like walking the nose, hanging ten, fast turns and pullouts, and fast takeoffs became possible with the balsa boards. Very popular at the surfing beach at Malibu, the balsa board was nicknamed the "Malibu" board.

Balsa had certain disadvantages. The wood still became waterlogged if the glass cover was fractured, and finding sufficient high-quality balsa was always a problem for the builder. Balsa boards were also difficult to fabricate and most of the work of shaping the wood was done by hand. Anyone visiting a surfboard shop ten years ago would have had to kick his way through bushel after bushel of balsa shavings.

Modern plastic technology gave surfing its biggest boost with the development of polyurethane foams. Boards could be molded, colors could be added to the laminating resins, and semi-mass-production became possible. Today a plastic company in Ventura, California, is turning out semi-custom-made boards by the thousands, and they are sold all over the world.

Surfing has gone big time. Like skin diving, golf, sports cars, and sky diving, surfing now has an established place in American recreational life. All along both coasts of the United States, people are shouldering foam and fiberglass planks and marching down to the sea. Inland the sport of wake surfing has created a demand for boards and boats to make surf. Young Frenchmen are sliding waves at Biarritz, and Chileans and Peruvians and South Africans have all the surf they need. Englishmen now surf at Singapore and on their home island, and almost everywhere, the young of mind and strong of back seek surf.

Hawaii Visitors Bureau

All it takes is trunks, guts and skill.

There are more facets to surfing than the sliding of a wood or plastic board across the face of a wave. Surfing, in its broadest meaning, includes any activity that can be done along a beach and in breaking waves. Add a prefix to surfing and we have:

Body Surfing. Sliding waves with the body instead of a board can be enjoyed at most ocean beaches throughout the world. Body surfing is perhaps the purest form of wave riding. Nothing separates rider and wave. Body surfing can be as simple as a straight-ahead ride on a two-foot wave, or as thrilling as shooting along a fifteen-foot break at nearly the same direction and speed obtained by a board.

Mat Surfing. An adventuresome rider with a rubber surf mat can do just about any trick a conventional surfer can do. Mat surfing is especially enjoyable for children because mats can be ridden on very small waves. Air-filled pillowcases or mattress covers are two possible variations of mat surfing.

Boat Surfing. Dories, canoes, sailing catamarans, and a few special motorboats can be surfed by experts where waves break far from shore and spill gradually forward.

Bellyboard Surfing. An enjoyable ride can be had with a small wooden or plastic board about the size of an adult's chest. Right slides, left slides, and fast straight-ahead rides are easily made with a bellyboard.

Skim Boarding. A skim board is a round or oval piece of plywood that is slid along the shallows at the water's edge. The rider tosses the disc ahead of him and then jumps aboard. Fast rides of many yards are possible after a little practice.

Wake Surfing. Surfable waves can be generated by a powerboat. Inlanders can surf on any body of water where a good-size outboard motorboat will operate.

The growing popularity of surfing has caused this individualistic activity to become more and more organized. The congestion at surfing beaches created a need for some form of control. Beaches are being divided into separate surfing and swimming areas. Surfing is limited to certain hours at some beaches and banned altogether at others. To represent the interests of surfers, the United States Surfing Association (USSA) has been established. Clubs have been forming rapidly and regional and international competitions are being held more and more frequently. The annual December Makaha Surfing Contest in Hawaii is the equivalent to the world's championship of surfing. Surfers travel from the mainland, Australia and Peru every winter to compete at Makaha. Before long, Frenchmen, South Africans and other international surfers will be arriving at Makaha. There is already a strong movement to include surfing in the Olympic Games.

The United States Surfing Association is the counterforce to the bad reputation and publicity that some rowdy younger people have given surfing. These delinquents are responsi ble for the ban on surfing at several beaches and for the growing hostility of beach cities to visiting surfers. The USSA is attempting to save many of the present surfing areas for use by responsible surfers. The USSA has also stressed water safety and was the first organization to sponsor a Surf Clinic. The clinic teaches young beginners safety and helps them develop constructive attitudes of good sportsmanship and

Competitive tandem surfing on long stable tandem boards—1963 Huntington Beach, California, Surfing Championships.

Ron Church

responsibility. Information concerning the United States Surfing Association may be obtained by writing to: Box 342, Laguna Beach, California.

Besides organizations and teams and clubs, surfing has attracted moviemakers, both "purist" and Hollywood producers. The purists are surfers turned moviemakers. Their films appeal to a specialized audience—no story or love interest spoils the action of men on giant waves. These films are shown by the makers, who add personal narration. Most of the pure-surf filmmakers do a highly professional job. Cameramen-producers like John Severson and Bud Browne expose miles and miles of footage in order to present two hours of entertainment. People interested in surfing can learn a great deal about the more dramatic aspects of the sport from an evening at a surf film.

Hollywood producers add a standard plot of boy meets girl meets big wave with plenty of music and color. Several nationally distributed Hollywood surfing films have made their producers small fortunes, and more are planned.

Madison Avenue and the advertising profession haven't overlooked the surfing mystique in their battle for the consumer's attention. The image of surfing is used to sell everything from autos to soft drinks to instant-dry-non-fat-low-cal-good-for-mothers-and-surfers powdered milk. This is a good indication that surfing is here to stay.

Chapter 2

GETTING STARTED

LEARNING to surf involves much more than the physical act of paddling a surfboard, standing on a wave, and riding like a bronze god to shore. The surfer needs to understand something of basic oceanography, a little about marine life, tides and currents, effects of weather on surf and sea, and quite a bit about swimming and general watermanship. Four essentials are required before starting: basically sound body, swimming ability, waves, and a surfboard.

Health. Surfing is a strenuous sport that places great demands on the heart, the respiratory system, and the muscles. Brute strength is not required, but good health and a body that can be conditioned to take increased physical work are. Older people require more and slower conditioning to get in shape for surfing, but this is true of any sport. Children and young people respond to training quickly and their muscles and body tone rapidly develop to meet the demands of paddling and swimming. Perfect health and a 100 percent sound body are not absolutely essential, though they are helpful. (Several amputees have learned to surf. The late Bob Simmons, a great surfer and one of the sports pioneers, had a withered arm. A few of the top big-wave riders have bad eyesight, but they do very well with contact lenses.) The one prerequisite for surfing is the ability of the body to recover normally from fatigue. Every time the board is launched, paddled out, and returned on a wave, the arms and back and lungs get a terrific workout. If one cannot regain sufficient strength after brief rest periods, then surfing may be too strenuous. These rest periods become shorter and shorter with conditioning and practice. Being very tired at first is normal for the beginning surfer. Modern coaching methods tell us that athletes must train specifically for each sport. Track and field training won't help the gymnast, and long brisk walks won't condition the surfer's shoulder and back muscles. Prior exercise will make training easier, but there is no substitute for getting in the water and swimming and paddling.

Swimming. A surfer should be a strong swimmer. This means someone who can swim a half mile or more in rough water and still climb out on shore and stand up. The good swimmer need not have a competitive swimming background or even be a speed burner, but he should be comfortable in the water and sufficiently skillful to make the beach safely no matter what the water condition.

Big surf often creates hazardous rip currents and churning turbulent water. A surfer who has lost his board after a wipe-out may be taken hundreds of yards from shore by a rip current (sometimes called rip tide). If the surfer can't stay afloat for extended periods of time and can't swim at least a half mile, he is in trouble. Boat wake surfing is safer because boats stay in calm water and help is close at hand. However, anyone who enjoys water sports should take the time to develop into a strong swimmer. Otherwise, drowning is a constant and not unlikely possibility.

Waves. Surfing waves are formed either by winds blowing across the surface of the oceans or by the wake created by a powerboat. Wake surfing is just beginning to become popular and no one knows yet how far and fast this sport will develop. It may be that artificial wave machines will be starting surfers sliding all over the country in another ten years. It could happen. Or surfers might hook on the wake

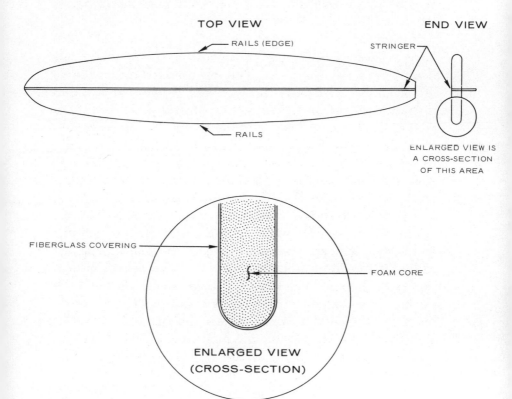

TOP VIEW

RAILS (EDGE)

RAILS

END VIEW

STRINGER

ENLARGED VIEW IS
A CROSS-SECTION
OF THIS AREA

FIBERGLASS COVERING

FOAM CORE

ENLARGED VIEW
(CROSS-SECTION)

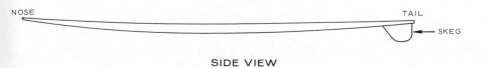

NOSE

TAIL

SKEG

SIDE VIEW

ANATOMY OF A MODERN SURFBOARD

DeGeneres

of giant oceangoing ships and ride their huge swells across the ocean—this will probably be tried too.

If pure, made-by-nature wave surfing is your goal, you'll have to visit an ocean beach, because the real variety just doesn't grow anywhere else. The surf does build to a couple of feet in the great lakes, but the wait between storms and the resulting surf might be months. Most exposed coastlines of the major oceans have surfable waves. Today more and more surfers are finding new places to surf, but the established areas are best for beginners. A few years ago Hawaii, Australia, and Southern California were the only places where surfers rode. Today the East Coast has opened up, and surfers are sliding from Long Island south to Florida.

The First Board. Most anything will do for paddling and getting in shape, but finding the right board for actual surfing is usually a problem unless you live near a custom surfboard shop and can have one tailor-made. Custom-built surfboards are expensive, but have good quality and workmanship. A reputable board builder designs and constructs a surfboard for the customer's individual size and weight, and the type of surf he'll normally ride. Top surfers and big-wave experts often have two boards, one for average-size waves (up to twelve feet) and one "big gun" board for large surf.

Pop-out boards are less expensive and more easily available. Pop-outs are mass-produced surfboards distributed through large sporting-goods and department stores. Many are of good quality, but some lack the strength and quality of a top-grade board. With mass-produced boards, it is difficult to distinguish good merchandise from junk. If the dealer is well known and offers a guarantee, then the board may be safe to buy. The fiberglass covering should be rigid, non-compressable and free of all blemishes. The skeg should be well beaded where it joins the tail of the board. This built-up area between the skeg and the bottom of the board makes the skeg stronger. Build-it-yourself-kit boards are also available and can be ordered directly from the dealer. Surfboard kits are shipped with all the necessary materials for building a board at home.

Used boards are widely available in California and Hawaii, but let the buyer beware. A good used board is expensive, often only a few dollars less than a new one. Since the integrity of a board depends on how well the glass covering holds the water out, there must be no cracks in the covering. A board that has been patched carefully is sound, but look out for a board that has recovered from major surgery and has whole sections grafted on.

The following chart will be useful in selecting the right size board.

Weight of Surfer	Length of Board	Width	Thickness
Under 100 lbs.	8' 9"	21½"	2¾"
100-120 lbs.	9'	22"	3"
120-150 lbs.	9' 6"	22"	3"
150-175 lbs.	9' 8" or 9' 10"	23"	3½"
175-200 lbs.	10' 0" or 10' 2"	23½"	4"
200 lbs. and over	10' 2" and over	24"	4"

These dimensions are all on the slightly oversize and buoyant side. A buoyant board, called a *floater*, is easier to handle. It paddles better and catches waves readily. A board too small for the surfer's weight tends to sink and is harder to paddle. If the board is too big, it paddles well, but is difficult to turn and control in a wave. If the board is too wide, it rubs the insides of the arms and make it difficult to dig in and take a full stroke when paddling.

Hazards and Safety. Anyone who has seen big Hawaiian winter surf will agree the huge waves look dangerous, and they are. Yet there have been few serious accidents among surfers. No one has yet compiled detailed statistics on surfing hazards, but unofficial sources list only ten to twelve drownings directly related to surfing between 1950 and 1964. Carelessness, inexperience, and too much daring all contribute to surfing accidents. Some principal dangers: a fast-moving board tangling with a crashing shorebreak wave; being skegged (run over); a pearling board shooting up in the air and coming down on its owner; washing into rocks or coral.

Surfing Fundamentals. A great deal can be learned by watching other surfers and the action of breaking waves, but observation doesn't develop balance and the fine points of surfing. The beginner should learn the basic techniques of paddling and board control before trying to catch the first wave. Without a good background of paddling, catching the first wave may become discouragingly hard. It takes a certain amount of skill to paddle a board out through a set of waves, spin it around and paddle again to catch a ride. Paddling is the best way to train for paddling, and paddling skillfully is half the battle of learning how to surf.

An expert paddler is able to get the most out of his board with the least expenditure of energy. The expert moves through the water faster, picks up a wave with only a few strokes and feels in balance either standing or paddling. Good board handling also adds to the safety of surfing. If the surfer caught in a set of big waves can paddle effectively he avoids being washed back or wiped out. If not, the waves win and he faces a swim back to shore.

Paddling a board is also an enjoyable sport in itself. Paddleboards have been in use as long as surfboards, and paddleboard races are held frequently on the West Coast and Hawaii. Years ago paddleboards and surfboards were almost identical but differences developed with advances in surfing technique and board design. Today there are three basic types of paddleboards in use: the long narrow racing board used in competition, the rescue paddleboard used by beach lifeguard services, and the classic round-nose, pointed-tail paddleboard for all-around use, known as the Blake board. The techniques of using paddleboard and surfboard are almost the same except for slight differences imposed by length and weight. Paddleboards are long, up to eighteen feet, and heavy; modern surfboards are seldom over ten feet in length and 35 pounds in weight. Techniques described here apply to both surfboard and general-purpose paddleboard.

Handling the Surfboard. Boards are awkward to transport, either by hand or by car. A board dropped on rock or pavement usually fractures; one dropped on a toe or foot will survive unscathed but the surfer may limp the rest of the day. Carrying a board along a crowded beach can cause problems, especially if the tail swings sideways and hits someone. If the board is carried at its center of balance and is always pointed ahead the tail won't swing sideways. Surfboards are carried under the arm, the hand and fingers curled around the lower rail. If the arm is too short for this, carry the board with the lower edge resting in the crook of the arm and the upper edge resting against the shoulder. Boards can also be carried on the head. A small towel placed between head and board makes this a comfortable alternative.

If the path to the beach is rocky and steep, take along a pair of tennis shoes. They'll save bruised feet and a dropped board. If the board is to be carried on top of the car, make sure it is tightly secured to the roof rack. Many such racks are available; some are dependable and some aren't. Test them carefully before use.

Waxing. Waxing the board can be done any time but seems to me more enjoyable at the beach under a warm sun that helps melt and spread the wax. Slipping is one of the major problems in paddling or riding a board. The smooth fiberglass covering becomes very slippery when wet. This is fine on the bottom of the board, but on the top it leads to fast wipe-outs and losing the board to the surf. Household canning paraffin is a simple solution for increasing traction on the top deck. The wax can be rubbed on, or melted and poured, or painted on with a brush. It takes a few minutes

Check the waves, other surfers and possible hazards. The white chalky coating on the board is paraffin to keep feet from slipping.

The prone position. Surfer's head is up, her upper body is raised off the board and her shoulders, back and arms all work together paddling. The board is well balanced. Note her fingers are loose and relaxed. There is no need to cup the hands.

Dick Gustafson

of hard rubbing to apply enough paraffin. *Cover the entire deck with wax.* A full coating gives the feet traction wherever they are placed and makes for a better hand grip in case you fall and grab for the board. Many surfers carry a small piece of wax in their trunks and wax their boards while waiting for a wave. When supply is short, wax the bottoms of your feet *instead of* the board.

Suntan oil, by the way, is disastrous on the surface of the board. The faintest trace of oil on the body is enough to make the board as slippery as butter in a skillet. Avoid using suntan oil before going surfing.

Launching the Board.   Select a path to the water away from rocks, cliffs, and other hazards. Check the shoreline for the following:

1. Is the bottom rocky or sandy?
2. Is there a drop into deeper water?
3. Will sea urchins or other marine animals such as barnacles or mussels cut and bruise feet?
4. Will breaking waves wash the board back?

A sandy bottom presents no problem, but it's difficult to wade out over rocks when slightly off balance due to carrying the board. Along rocky shore beaches, look for channels through which you can enter deeper water and can start paddling. If the surf is rolling into the shore and you must fight through the waves, wait for a calm period and then proceed quickly. Waves usually come in sets, and a few minutes' wait for the set to calm will spare you a wipe-out or a wash over the rocks. When wading over the rocks, turn the board upside down. This places the skeg in the air and keeps it from snagging on rocks on the way out. Some lightweights who float high on their board paddle over the rocks with the board upside down.

When walking out through small breaking surf, hold the board high and let the wave pass under it. Keep the nose of the board up; if it's pointed down the wave will wrest it from your grip. Always keep the board pointed straight ahead. If turned sideways when a wave hits, the board *broaches* (turns sideways and over) and is pulled away or washed back into you. Being struck by loose boards is no fun; regard them with caution. Being hit by your own adds insult to injury. If the board is pointed into the surf, it will probably punch through the wave and come through.

Paddling. The two paddling positions are the prone and the kneeling. The secret of paddling well lies in achieving good balance and using the muscles properly. On the board, try to find the exact center of balance quickly. Keep the weight of the body as much as possible over the center line of the board. The weight should also be placed so the nose of the board is just an inch or two above the level of the water. If the nose is too low, it will scoop up water and dig in; if it's too high, the tail will drag, create resistance, and the board will be hard to paddle. When the water is choppy, keep the nose slightly higher so water won't wash over it. If your body trips sideways, the board leans and will tip over with the slightest wave or slap of rough water. Hold your head high; keep a sharp lookout for waves—and other boards. Paddling out in good-size surf is a bit like running across a busy highway. Each wave can cause trouble, but if you know what is coming at you at all times, you can move ahead, go sideways, or retreat.

Prone Paddling. This position is the easiest to learn because the center of balance is low and the danger of tipping over is less. The chin-up position should be held for prone paddling because it helps arch the back so more muscles come into play when taking a stroke. When paddling, the arms, shoulders and back all work together. The combined efforts of these groups of muscles can drive a board surprisingly far and fast. Actually the body does not lie flat on the board. It is arched and the weight is carried on the lower chest, stomach and thighs. Most surfers paddle with one leg bent at the knee and the foot sticking up in the air. This natural body reaction helps maintain balance. The foot sticking up moves slightly from side to side, offsetting the tip of the board.

The paddling arm stroke is a natural overarm throw combined with dipping the hands and arms in the water and pulling back and through. Keep the fingers and the hands relaxed to reduce tension and tiredness. Paddling is a pull-recover-rest-pull cycle. The board glides ahead when the arms are recovered. The recovery is relaxed, giving the muscles time to rest. On a long paddle, alternate between work and rest by taking ten or more strokes, resting the arms on the board and letting it glide. The arm pull is firm with a quick recovery at the end of the stroke. Because the chest is raised and the back slightly arched, a deeper and stronger pull can be made. Some *feather* their hands after each stroke. Feathering is turning the hand parallel to the rails of the board to create less drag. Paddling is a sport in itself and competition paddlers have developed many techniques to increase efficiency. Paddlers in top condition take workouts of five miles and more. (Open-sea competition between Catalina Island and the California coast is held yearly.)

Knee Paddling. Once prone paddling is comfortable, try the knee position. This requires a little more balance, but if the board is not too narrow or tippy, knee paddling is easy. A lot of younger surfers seem to paddle only on their knees. It's really a matter of preference. Some surfers feel that a kneeling position is better for the takeoff due to the faster starts achieved.

Sit on your heels between strokes. When you paddle, the body rocks forward and the weight shifts from the center of balance forward to the nose. The hands dig in and the body is rocked back. Both the muscles and the momentum of the body rocking back add to the force of the stroke in the kneeling position. One advantage of a kneeling position on the takeoff is the quickness with which the center of balance can be changed. When paddling down the wave on the takeoff, it is sometimes necessary to move the balance point forward

Turning turtle—flipping the board—protects rider from onrushing wave.

set. There's no reason to waste energy fighting through broken surf when in a few minutes the sets of waves will diminish and a calm period will follow. Spot the best place to catch a wave, look for possible hazards, and judge the easiest way of getting outside. On some days, after a storm, for example, waves roll in continuously with no period of calm, or lull, between sets. On such days try to find a channel of calmer water to paddle out through. At most surfing beaches it is also possible to paddle around the break. At beaches where the surf humps up due to a rocky point or reef there is an area of calm water on one side of the break. It's better to try going around the break than paddling through it. Going around the end takes less fight, reduces the chance of getting hit by another board, and is quicker than a direct route out.

If it is impossible to get around the surf on days when it's breaking big and rough, you must gut it through. Waves often roll in at fifteen or twenty miles an hour. To bust through the advancing white water (the *soup*) the board must be paddled fast enough and with sufficient momentum to meet the shock of the wave without being pushed back. Just before smashing into the wave, rise to a push-up position. This posture allows the water to pass between the body and the board. As waves grow bigger (over four feet) you will be unable to develop sufficient thrust to overcome the shock of the wave. In such situations, use the board itself as protection from the crashing surf by *turning turtle*. This means flipping the board over you and hanging on while the wave passes overhead. If the surf is large, wrap the legs and arms around the board. The body hanging to the board acts as a sea anchor and keeps the board from being washed back too far by the force of the wave. Having the board overhead is also protection from other boards coming down at you from any angle. It's a rough haul to fight through six or seven waves, paddle hard, and then go turtle again and again. Good physical condition pays off here.

Chapter 3

BEGINNING SURFING TECHNIQUES

THE beginner should surf at the less crowded beaches or during the hours before or after the crowds. Surfing is great in the early morning, when waves are smooth and unruffled by the later day winds. Along many beaches the wind drops off in the evening and surfing can be especially enjoyable near sunset if the air is warm. Don't keep surfing until dark. When the light fades, it becomes difficult to judge distances and the chances for wipe-outs increase.

On densely surfed beaches and on days when swells are arriving in sets, wait for the last wave and then get a ride after the other surfers have ridden in. The last waves of a set sometimes produce a smooth, fast ride because the preceding waves have piled into shore and flattened the surface of the water. Some days the sets will be so consistent that their arrival can be timed to the minute.

The First Ride

Let's create an imaginary surfer and follow him through the steps of catching a wave. To give our fictitious friend a personality, call him Barney and give him enough skill in paddling and swimming so that he's safe in the water. Barney has played it smart and arrived at the beach early in the morning. There are only six or seven surfers out on the water and the surf is perfect, not large, but well formed and coming in consistently. Barney has been waiting for this morning for several weeks and there's an exciting feel about the day and what's to come. As Barney is spreading a good nose-to-tail coat of paraffin on his board, he hears one of the surfers yell, *"Outside."* Barney looks up and sees a good set of swells rolling into the bay. The surfers spin their boards around and get into position. Barney notices that the wave will form a right shoulder and the surfers will be sliding right. (When describing direction or slide or break it is always from the surfers' point of view, not from the beach point of view.) The surfers all start paddling together and all but one begin to slide. Together they stand and turn away from the breaking shoulder of the wave. Too many are on the same wave and they begin to jam up. One cuts back over the top and the rest fight for a good position. Three boards collide, two riders go down and the others ride on. The riderless boards bounce in on the white water and drift into the rocks. Barney wants to be a "good guy" and trots into the water to grab a loose board. A little wave he didn't notice hits the floating board. Before Barney can jump aside the loose board smacks him across the ankles. Retreating Barney digests an important lesson: *Keep away from free-floating boards and never stand directly in front of one.* This safety rule goes for anything heavy that's washing in on a wave. Now Barney approaches the board again and takes it on the side where a wave can't wash it into him. He shoves it seaward to its rider who waves thanks. Barney then turns around to grab his own board. It's missing! Who took it? Nobody but a wave that washed up higher than the rest and floated his board out on the backwash. Barney retrieves it and reflects, *Better not leave my board, or anything else, where the surf and high tide can get it.*

Barney wades out to where the water is deep enough to paddle and drops his board in. He jumps on, assumes the kneeling position and paddles out, carefully adjusting his balance so the board isn't tippy. He goes around the far end, giving incoming surfers a wide berth. The surf isn't large, so there's no problem of paddling outside. When he's out to where the break starts he stops his board, sits back and takes a look around. He's in a fine spot, slightly to the side of the other surfers and close enough to the breaking waves to catch one. He says hello to another surfer, gets a half smile in response and then everyone looks out to sea.

Now the waiting game begins. In surfing it's always hurry out and wait for a wave. Most days the wait will be just long enough to rest tired muscles; but there are bad days when the surf doesn't show and after you've given up and paddled in to the beach the one set of the day comes in. But today Barney is lucky. A set is coming and each surfer is judging in his own mind the best place to be when the wave arrives. Barney turns his board shoreward and gets set. He's all alone now and his stomach is tense with anticipation. The wave comes swiftly and the other surfers start to paddle, but it's not big enough where Barney waits so he lets it pass by. As the shorebound swell lifts him up he sees other waves coming. Here is his chance; if the others take the first waves the last one will be all his. Barney has thought out this first wave in advance—he is not going to try standing the first time; he'll ride it on his knees. He wants to get the "feel" of a slide.

The swells arrive, hit shallow water, turn into surf and roll toward the beach. The others stand and ride in and Barney is left with the whole bay to himself. Coming straight for him is his wave. It looks huge but Barney knows it's his and he's got to try for it. The time to paddle is now and Barney digs in and sends his board flying. He is starting straight off. The wave is directly behind him and his board is at right angles to it. Barney glances over his shoulder to judge what the wave is doing. He sees white water starting off to his left side, but far enough away so he knows it won't crash on him. If the wave were about to collapse there would still be time to pull out—stopping the board by sitting back on the tail. But everything looks GO and he digs in with one final strong pull. The swell comes, the nose of the board tips down, the tail rises and he begins to slide. This is the thrill of the start, the slide, the sense of motion that says you're starting your ride and the energy of the sea and surf has caught you and is yours to master. At this precise moment Barney feels the thrill of surfing—he's in a wave and his board is sliding by wave force alone.

Having caught the wave, Barney remembers to turn and lean away from the breaking portion. It's like flying. Almost without thinking he goes to his knees and leans farther into the wave. Now it seems terribly steep. White water is breaking over the back of the board, spray is spitting in his eyes, and Barney loses control. The wave collapses, hundreds of gallons of water pour over him, and in a twinkle of a second his board is torn away. Barney pops up through the soup sputtering, looking wildly about for other boards and then, realizing he's safe, yells inwardly: "I did it!"

Barney's board has washed in to the beach. It's his first wipe-out and now he has to swim for his board. This is something surfers will do again and again. It's all part of the game. Today the swells are not large, but there is enough force in them to help him get back to the beach. Barney notices that after each wave passes there is a shoreward pull. He swims harder when this pull comes, letting the passing waves help him. As each wave comes toward him Barney looks carefully for other surfers or loose boards. It is the responsibility of the rider to watch out for the swimmer, but Barney is still ready to *dive for the bottom* if a board comes too close.

Back on the beach Barney finds his board and paddles out again. The surf is picking up now. He plans to paddle around the break, but one set starts to break right in front of him. Barney digs in harder, paddling to meet the wave with enough force to keep from being knocked back. The wave comes and he turns turtle for the first time. He grips his

Allan Walker

Ride your first wave on the knees or prone to get the feel of surfing. The board is in good trim and the nose is raised to prevent pearling.

Riding the soup. This surfer rode straight off the break into the white water. He makes sure the nose of the board stays up to prevent pearling. Notice how the tail of the board is buried and the rider's weight is back.

board tightly and rolls over. The shock of the wave almost rips the board from him, but he holds on and the wave passes by. Now he paddles even harder, trying to move out far enough to get over the next wave before it breaks. It's close but he makes it. Just to be sure he doesn't get washed back again, he continues paddling until he is safely beyond the point where the biggest waves are breaking.

In the takeoff spot Barney decides he will pick his wave and ride it all the way in. He's going to experiment and see if he can get his board to stay in front of the breaking part of the wave. He knows by riding as close to parallel as possible to the wave front his board will go faster. The water in front of him is clear of surfers and he's ready to go. A good-sized wave comes and Barney knee-paddles to catch it.

He looks back quickly to check the wave. It has already started breaking on one side. He realizes that this wave is critical and starts his turn while paddling. The wave lifts his board and he begins to slide. He leans farther into the wave and the board turns faster. Now the wave starts breaking on both sides of Barney and in an instant white water will be all around him. He doesn't want to lose his board this time so he decides to ride the soup in and save himself from a wipe-out. Barney shifts his weight again to head straight toward the beach. Next he slides his weight back to raise the nose of the board and keep it from pearling. The soup surrounds him but Barney hangs on and gets a straight-off bouncy ride to the beach.

This ride wasn't the way Barney planned it, but he did retain his board and make it to the beach. On this wave Barney noticed that slight changes of balance on the takeoff might mean catching the wave or not. *Too far forward causes pearling; too far back causes stalling.* He also learned to recover from a possible wipe-out by turning back into the wave and shifting his weight to the back of the board. The nose should be kept high when riding straight off to prevent pearling. When Barney saw that the wave was starting to collapse in front of him, he could have pulled out by dropping over the back of the wave and letting it pass by. This is done by a rapid shift of weight to the tail of the board and an extreme turn into the face of the wave. The pullout is a basic part of surfing and should be practiced often. There are many styles of pullouts, but for the beginner it is enough to learn the sharp turn coupled with stalling the board. This type of pullout will raise the nose of the board and allow it to go over the top of the wave at the same time the stern is pivoting.

The most important thing Barney learned on his first few rides was the exciting feeling of the takeoff and slide. He now knows what to expect next time and can pay more attention to form and style. Many basic skills can be learned riding prone or kneeling. Don't feel self-conscious surfing this way at first. Other surfers, looking so great now, also went through the learning experience. Having caught the first few waves either prone or kneeling, the new surfer can then try turning quicker; taking off closer to the breaking portion of the wave; and seeing how changes in balance affect the board. If the board is allowed to get too low on the wave, it is hard to control. Riding the wave near the top permits a faster pullout if the wave begins to collapse.

Many new surfers try too hard at first and become tired quickly due to lack of conditioning and experience. It's best to take a short rest after paddling back out. While the arms rest and the breath returns to normal, get in position for the next wave. But if you're really exhausted head for the beach and a good rest. Cold and fatigue mean wasted effort, missed waves, and frequent wipe-outs. A tired body just won't respond to the demands of surfing.

Standing

Standing up on the board can be done at any time during the initial part of the ride. Experts get to their feet quickly, turn the board at the right moment, and slide away. The beginner may want to wait until the board is turned and riding smoothly before standing. Many beginners jump to their feet too soon causing the board to stall out or nose down and pearl. Trying to catch a wave that's too small or one without enough slope is also a waste of energy. Younger or new surfers often get crowded out of the best surfing spots and become discouraged when they miss wave after wave. In this case it's either fight for a good spot or surf when or where crowds are smaller.

To stand, either come directly to the feet in one smooth motion or rise to the knees or a crouch and then stand up. Most surfers take a standing position with the left leg forward and the right foot back. Some reverse this stance and earn the name of *goofy-foot*. It's the back leg that transmits changes of body balance to the board. The farther back the weight is placed and the greater the lean toward the face of the wave, the faster the board will turn. An extreme movement of this type will produce the pullout. Moving the

Three stages of standing up. The surfer at left is still on his knees; the one in the middle pushes himself up, and the surfer at right is rising.

weight forward toward the nose will drop it until it digs in and pearls. This is another type of pullout. A carefully balanced forward position will result in the best speed, but it is hard to maintain. In the basic stand-up position the feet are usually spread about one and a half feet apart and the rear foot is turned almost at right angles to the center line of the board. The body can face directly forward or be turned about 45° off the center line. The standing position varies with the individual surfer. Many different positions are used, depending on the wave, the man, and the surf condition. Practice will help determine which position is best for the individual.

Chapter 4

WAVES AND SURFING

FOR thousands of years seafarers have known that waves are born from the wind blowing across the surface of the sea. Only in recent years has oceanography revealed just how complex the process of wave motion is. Though ocean waves are created by winds, the gravitational pull of the moon and sun also creates small, almost indiscernible waves. These are true *tidal* waves as opposed to waves caused by seismic disturbances. Oceanographers have yet to decide what to call either the destructive seismic-produced waves or the everyday tide-produced, relatively slow-moving wave. Changes in barometric pressure, depth of water and bottom topography also have their effect on waves. Winds blowing from different directions create a confused wave pattern. The speed of winds and their duration and direction also affect how waves are formed and how they finally come to subside on the beach.

The principal oceans of the world extend thousands of miles between the coasts of major land masses. These long stretches of open water enable the energy of the wind to be absorbed by water. This mating of wind and water produces waves. But before a wave picks up the tail of a surfboard and starts its rider sliding shoreward the wind must have satisfied three important conditions. 1) The wind must blow over the water with sufficient velocity to start the surface water in motion. 2) The wind must blow for a sufficient length of time in a constant direction, and 3) The wind must blow over a long distance of open water.

A wave begins to form when the first gentle breezes brush the surface of the water. The breeze must contain enough energy to start ripples. Each small ripple is like a tiny sail for the wind to push upon. As the wind continues to blow against its back, the ripple grows bigger and moves faster. Since winds are normally gusty and do not blow with 100 percent consistency, the ripples begin to diffuse and become irregular. As the velocity of the wind increases these ripples build in size and finally become waves. As the waves grow bigger and the wind continues to rise, the tops of the waves fall over, or are blown off, and whitecaps form. Whitecaps are seen on any body of water when strong local winds blow. But these local winds do not produce swells. How then are the large ocean-traveling swells that make surfing possible created?

The Anatomy of a Wave

The distance a swell travels from its creation by the winds to its breakup on shore is called the *fetch*. The highest point of the wave is named the *crest*, and the lowest portion is the *trough*. Waves are also said to have length, *wavelength* being distance between two crests. The longer the wavelength the more energy it can absorb from the wind and the greater its *height*. This is why the fetch is so important. A fetch of 600 to 800 miles is needed for large swells to develop. Old sailors guessed almost correctly that wave height is about half the speed of the wind. For example, winds of 60 miles per hour produce open sea waves 30 feet high. The speed at which waves travel is directly proportional to wave height. If the speed of waves is increased by 50 percent their height will increase by 50 percent. If both height and speed increase by one-half, the distance between individual waves will increase by a factor of 100 percent.

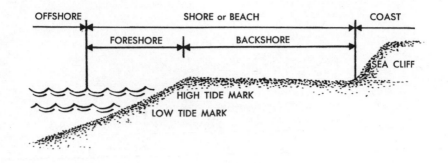

OFFSHORE   SHORE or BEACH   COAST

FORESHORE   BACKSHORE

SEA CLIFF

HIGH TIDE MARK

LOW TIDE MARK

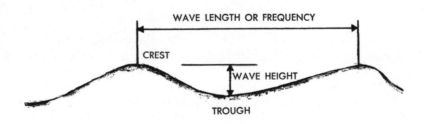

WAVE LENGTH OR FREQUENCY

CREST

WAVE HEIGHT

TROUGH

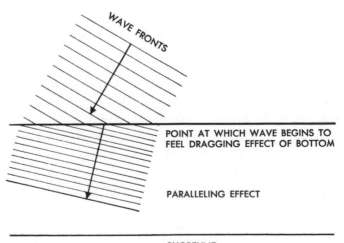

WAVE FRONTS

POINT AT WHICH WAVE BEGINS TO
FEEL DRAGGING EFFECT OF BOTTOM

PARALLELING EFFECT

SHORELINE

An overwhelming wave about to cover a U. S. Coast Guard 44-foot steel lifeboat. The waves that pound over the bar at Newport Harbor, Oregon, begin their march shoreward from thousands of miles away in the West Pacific. Incidentally, the lifeboat made it.

Surfers talk endlessly about big waves and rides on towering giants. Old-time surfers are especially prone to recount their rides to new surfers. Stories usually begin: "Back in the big storm of '38 the waves were . . ." Some of these tall wave tales are true, and some of them grow with time.

Here's one big wave story that is true and hard to beat. The story was documented in the *Proceedings of the U. S. Naval Institute* and in Rachel Carson's absorbing book, *The Sea Around Us*. A U. S. Navy tanker, the USS *Ramapo*, was outbound from Manila en route to San Diego the winter of 1933. The tanker's captain, Lt. Commander R. P. Whitemarsh, anxiously watched severe storm conditions develop for several days. In the ship's log he recorded winds of 30 to 50 knots blowing steadily during this time. The barometer began falling and bounced close to bottom at 29.29 inches. As the winds continued to blow, giant swells developed. The tanker was sailing with the winds to her stern, the only possible safe direction in the huge seas. Luckily the *Ramapo* was a big tanker of 478 feet and took the swells steadily. At the height of the storm one of the lookouts on the bridge glanced astern and saw a tremendous wave overtaking them. At this instant the bow inclined steeply up the face of the wave and its stern sank in the trough. From where the lookout stood on the bridge, he was at the same level as the crow's nest. To his horrified surprise, the swell rose up higher than the crow's nest and loomed over the ship. The wave did not crest and passed them by. Later, with the aid of simple geometry, the captain calculated that the wave was at least 112 feet high. Its speed was approximately 55 knots. Can any of your surfing friends top this?

The waves created by storms at sea are violent confused beasts that roll, crest, and break haphazardly. After a storm has passed, the swells generated by it continue to move in the direction the storm blew. When the violent winds subside, the swells begin to change, settling down and becoming lower and more uniform. Resembling the rounded swells that finally arrive at the beach, they are now *rolling swells* (often called ground swells). The energy they absorbed from the wind keeps them traveling until they reach a land mass.

Waves that have come a considerable distance, and arrive in sets, indicate that storms have raged thousands of miles away. Waves reaching the California shore in the summer usually come from the south and may have originated as far away as New Zealand in the South Pacific. On the Atlantic Coast waves are of a shorter period and much choppier. This is because Atlantic storms occur much closer to shore and the swells have no time to smooth over a long fetch. Swells rolling in from the South Atlantic have better form due to the longer distance traveled before reaching shore.

Swells move across the surface of the open sea at an average speed of 12 to 15 knots per hour. Surface swells disturb only the upper layers of the ocean leaving the deeper water unaffected. Recent studies reveal that underwater swells, or waves, occur, but how they are generated is unknown. The life of the swell is never certain. Many never reach shore. Some are destroyed by winds which flatten them or change their direction. Rain, hail and snow reduce the intensity of a swell.

From the beach a wave appears to be one large mass of advancing water, but this is not really so. If this huge wall of water did actually move, the earth would be inundated. Waves don't really move masses of water along; it is the wave form that moves, *through* the water. Watch an object floating on the surface of the water. When the swell comes and passes by, the object moves only slightly shoreward. It is the wave form moving through the water that moves the object. There is also a countermotion backward if the swell is steep enough.

When the swell passes, it sets the water in motion in an orbital circle. If we could put a giant glass tank in the ocean and stand in it, we could observe this phenomenon clearly by watching the effect of the passing swell on fine sand particles. The movement of each sand particle is shoreward in its orbit. The size of orbit is equal to the height of the wave. When the sand particles reach the top of the orbit (at the crest), they move forward in the direction the swell is running. This orbital motion of water decreases with depth until it disappears altogether.

Surf

We have seen that swells are formed by the winds and when they reach land they run in long parallel rows. Now—what makes swells turn into surf?

When swells meet the coast, or anything that obstructs them, they lose their energy and change shape. Swells begin the process of becoming surf when the depth of water is shallower than one-half the distance from crest to crest—the wavelength. As the swells roll into shallow water, the bottoms of the orbiting swells are slowed by the drag, or friction, of the bottom. The waves begin to pile up as the bottom of the surface wave slows and the top portion proceeds at full force. Since the bottom of the wave is slowing down, crests begin to peak and the wave becomes steeper. When it becomes so steep that the face of the wave can no longer support it, the crest topples forward into the trough. This is surf, and this is what we wait and hope for.

Waves start breaking when the depth of the water is approximately one and one-third of their height. For example, a three-foot wave will break in four-foot-deep water and a nine-foot wave will break in twelve-foot-deep water.

The foregoing demonstrates why smaller waves break closer to shore and larger waves farther out. This is the normal pattern for surf at a normal beach, but as any surfer or sailor knows, waves don't always behave normally. Add a little offshore wind to help hold the wave face up and it will come closer to the beach before breaking.

Three kinds of break are of interest to surfers: reef break, point break, and shore break. These produce either a *crasher* or a *roller*. A crasher dumps all at once so that tons of water fall forward and smash into the sand or rocks. Crashers, pounders, plungers, sand busters—all these terms denote heavy shorebreak or waves that collapse suddenly. *Rolling surf* means waves that begin breaking at the crest and spill forward gradually. The best example of rolling or spilling surf can be found at Waikiki Beach, Hawaii, where long swells break very smoothly and roll forward over the shallow bottom.

Reef Break. Reef break produces some of the most exciting surf known. Famous surfing areas like Sunset Beach, Bonzai Pipeline, and Avalanche in Hawaii and San Onofre and Wind and Sea in California are typical reef break surf spots. Surfing a reef break area has certain unique advan-

Commerce Department, U. S. Coast and Geodetic Survey

Aerial shot of surf breaking over coral reef near Kahului Harbor, Maui Island, Hawaii. The swells and breaking surf follow the curve of the beach. The break in the surfline indicates either a deep channel or a large rip current.

tages. Usually there is a deep-water stretch between the reef and the shore. This depressed bottom condition between the beach and the reef keeps the surf from collapsing suddenly and produces longer and more stable waves. As mentioned earlier, waves begin breaking when the depth of water is one and one-third times the height of the wave. Of course if the water becomes too deep on the shore side of the reef the wave will flatten and become a swell again, and the surfer will lose the steep wave face to ride on. The shape of the bottom also helps determine just how the wave will break and what form it will hold as it rolls shoreward. A reef that rises sharply toward the surface in the center and gradually drops off at each end produces waves that have both a left and right shoulder to ride on. A reef with a deep depression somewhere along its span will have a calmer area bordered by surf. Changes in underwater reef level often aid the surfer by creating channels of quieter water to paddle out through. Experienced surfers usually take a long look for these channels before paddling out.

A deep-water reef will start the swells breaking only when the swell height is nearly equal to the depth of the reef. A reef that is close to the surface causes large swells to break haphazardly, which ruins their form for surfing. An example of deep reef break is Harrison's Reef in California, which is about eight to ten feet deep on a high tide and almost a half mile from shore. When large winter swells of eight feet or more come rolling onto this reef, excellent surfing waves are produced. If the swells are small they do not form waves. Between the reef and the shore, the bottom deepens, and the swells, unless large, flatten out—and the surfer finds himself without a ride.

The reef at Wind and Sea in Southern California produces left and right shoulders for the surfer to slide in either direction. The top of the reef is broad and once the waves start breaking they hold up until reaching shore.

On the east coast of the United States sand bars often

build up offshore. Between the sandbars and the beach lies
an area of deep water. If the Atlantic swells are large and
consistent and the water deep enough, good surf forms over
the sandbars. Sandbars usually run for some distance and
are quite even in depth. This type of topography produces
spillers that break from the top and roll gradually forward.
Right and left slides are not unusual. Because of the gradual
break, the surfer usually rides straight off in the *soup* (white
water) as he slides shoreward. Sandbar formations change
rapidly due to the effects of storms and currents. A good
surfing area might build overnight where none previously
existed, or a good spot might vanish. One sand beach in
California was cut back over twenty yards in one night by
the action of currents. Since oceans and shorelines are in a
constant state of flux, surfers must regard each day individually and plan accordingly.

Point Break. This type of break is formed by a point of
land that juts seaward. Such protrusions of land into sea

cause incoming swells to bend, or refract shoreward as they advance into shallower water around the point of land. This refraction effect is similar to light passing through a denser medium such as glass or water. The refraction of swells makes them draw more closely to shore, and the wave speed is subsequently reduced. The degree of bottom slope and the extent of the point's land mass help determine the final form the wave will take.

Surfrider Beach at Malibu, California, and Makaha Beach, Hawaii, are examples of point break surf. The Malibu Beach is really a point plus a reef. The head of land sticking out into the Pacific causes the incoming swells to refract and the reeflike bottom at Malibu ascends so gradually that the waves roll in for a considerable distance before breaking. At Malibu large swells coming in from a southwesterly direction produce ideal surfing conditions and waves of perfect form. Extremely long rides are possible if the shoreline behind a point is long, the bottom slopes gradually to shallow

Reef break, Hawaii. The drag of the reef causes the shorebound swell to break in the center. On this wave both a left and right shoulder were formed. Surfer in center has pearled and is half a second away from a wipe-out. The nose of his board is down and under water.

Ron Church

water and the swells parallel the beach to some degree. Even a small point of land will help form surfable waves. A jetty, breakwater or even the hull of a sunken ship resting in shallow water will serve the same purpose by refracting swells and starting them to crest.

Shorebreak. During the era of the long wood boards and straight-ahead surfing styles, riding shorebreak was completely ignored. The old boards just couldn't turn, which meant riding shorebreak was a sure wipe-out. The short modern fast-turning Malibu board makes riding shorebreak possible. Surfers can safely take off in a fast collapsing wave, get a short swift ride and pull out of the wave before it closes over them. Shorebreak is what the name implies, waves that break close to shore.

There is a difference between surfable shorebreak and sand-busting crashers. Shorebreak surf retains enough wave face for a fast ride of short duration. Sand busters just collapse suddenly upon reaching shore and shouldn't be ridden due to the danger of severe wipe-out. Most accidents occur in the shorebreak due to rapid loss of board control and violent contact with the shallow bottom. Shorebreak surf results from swells entering shallow water, reacting to the frictional effect of the bottom, steepening quickly and then spilling forward and breaking. Beaches with surfable shorebreak have a gradually descending bottom. The degree of slope must be gentle enough to create a forward-rolling wave instead of a crasher. Wave shoulders will be formed if some portions of the bottom are steeper than others. The degree of swell direction will also influence how each wave will form, roll forward and exhaust itself. If the direction of the incoming swell is bent from the horizontal line of the beach, the waves will start breaking at one end instead of across the whole line of the swells. This is because the most shoreward portion of the swell encounters shallow water first and begins cresting. If this is the case, a shoulder will form on the unbroken portion of the wave and better rides are

A two-mile-high aerial photograph shows wave refraction on a point of land. Note how the swells diminish upon entering the protected bay —Cordova, Alaska.

possible. As in reef break and point break surf, knowing the area will help the surfer pick the best spot for the takeoff and slide.

Sometimes a ride in the shorebreak will be abruptly terminated when the rider encounters a strong *backwash*. Backwash is the result of water flowing down the slope of a beach after a wave has spent itself. Backwash can also be classified as a reflected wave. The steeper the slope the faster the water will rush down. If this outrush of water meets an incoming wave, the two forces oppose each other, and the water is forced skyward. If the backwash and incoming wave both contain great energy, a rather spectacular geyser is formed. Surfers who ride into the beach and stay with their boards until the last possible moment sometimes meet the backwash. The upheaval is strong enough at times to hurl surfer and board several feet in the air. The backwash usually develops in shallow water, and to be caught in this turmoil can be dangerous.

The downward rush of water characteristic of the backwash has sometimes been called, incorrectly undertow. This is because of the sensation of being swept seaward by the outrushing water that cascades down a sloping beach. A man being swept down the slope is really not being pulled under, but is being moved along by the natural rush of water down an incline. The wave that breaks over him completes the illusion of being towed under.

At some beaches strong shorebreak and backwash produce *gutter rips*. These are caused by small valleylike depressions in the sand along the water's edge. As the surf rolls up the beach it drains into the depressions as well as retreats back to sea. The depressions or gullies then contain much more water than originally washed into them. The water sweeping down the gutters is like a small swift river, and its outward speed can be very fast. Gutter rips are especially dangerous to children, who are easily swept off their feet and out to sea. Several years ago along one beach heavily convoluted by gutter rips, five beach lifeguards rescued over fifty children in a half-mile stretch—in less than two hours.

Shorebreak surfing is an exciting fast-moving game. Wipe-outs happen with split-second speed and the hard sand of the shallow bottom is always waiting. Riding the shorebreak is not for beginners, but with experience it can be a thrilling part of surfing.

Tidal Waves

Though not a problem to surfers as vehicles to ride, tidal waves are of great general interest, and understanding how they occur is a part of basic ocean knowledge.

Most tidal waves (sometimes called *tsunamis*) occur in the Pacific, originating from seismic disturbances along the rim of the ocean. Mammoth earthquakes in places such as the Aleutian Trench of Alaska generate waves that travel great distances at extremely high speeds. When huge portions of the sea floor or edge are moved by an earthquake, massive amounts of water are displaced which surge upward, or downward, form waves, and move radially from the point of origin. Such waves have remarkably long length— a mile or more between crests; and speeds may average 400 or more miles per hour. But the tidal wave becomes destructive only when it reaches shallow water. In the deeper part of the ocean, there is no rush of white water or breaking wave; a ship in deep water would be wholly unaffected by a passing tidal wave. A severe tsunami struck Hawaii in April 1946. The captain of a ship riding outside Hilo watched the series of giant waves smash into the island, but his ship, standing in very deep water, never felt a single effect of the wave.

Signs of tidal waves register on seismographs throughout the world. Without these warnings the only indication that a tidal wave is at hand is a sudden radical lowering of the water level, as if the low tide of all time had occurred. During the Chilean and Alaskan earthquakes very strong tidal surges caused damage along the California coast, though no large waves struck. If you're sitting on your surfboard in six or eight feet of water and suddenly the skeg of your board hits bottom, it might be a good idea to paddle in and look for high ground.

Tides and Surfing

The phenomenon of the cyclic rhythmic rise and fall of the water level along most coasts of the world results from the gravitational pull of the moon and sun. High tide is the maximum height reached by each rising of the cycle and low tide is the minimum height reached by the falling tide. Technically the term *tide* refers only to the vertical movement of the water. *Tidal currents* are the horizontal movements of the water. For example, the extremely swift flow of water in and out of the deep narrow fjords of Norway is caused by tidal current. The tide period is the interval from low tide to the next recurrent low tide or from high tide to the next recurrent high tide. Tidal periods vary in different parts of the world, but twelve hours and twenty-five minutes is the normal interval in most places. Tides are said to advance each day. The tidal advance also varies. For example, high tide might fall at 12 noon on one day, 12:45 the next day and 1:22 the following day. The normal advance of the tide is somewhere between forty and sixty minutes per cycle, but exact prediction of expected tides in any one location must be based upon years of observation of tidal heights and timing at that location. The *range* of the tide is the difference between high and low water. Tidal range varies greatly between different locations throughout the world. Along the normal open coast the tidal variations range between three feet and eight feet. In some unusual bays the tidal variation may be as great as fifty feet. The famous Bay of Fundy experiences such tides. Ships entering this bay only have a few minutes to tie up, unload and proceed out. Those that remain are left high and dry when the tide rushes out.

After being around the shore for a while, surfers begin to recognize the tidal effects on surfing at different beaches. With a background of wave watching, and a book of tide tables, you can predict surf conditions at different beaches. If you know the approximate height of the prevailing swells, the type of beach you plan to surf at, and the height of the tide (all this information can be obtained by calling the local lifeguard service or the Coast Guard), a good prediction of the surf is possible. For example, consider a group of surfers who plan to make a journey of several hours to a surfing beach. They arrive at the coast and have to make a decision: will surf be up and is it worthwhile to continue the long drive? One points out that the swells are coming in from the right direction to make for a good break at the beach they're heading for. Another remarks it will be high tide when they reach their destination (they know their beach is a high-tide surfing area). They make a decision: the surf will be good at high to medium tide, and the trip will be worth the effort. Had they decided the tide would be low, they would have altered their plans and visited another beach.

Chapter 5

SURF SAFETY

SURFING does something to a person after a while. It becomes a challenge, or a skill to perfect, or even a way of life. Surfers, after learning the basic fundamentals, begin looking for bigger and faster waves, new places to surf, and new ways to express themselves on a wave. There seems to be a pressure to push on and become better and better. This means more and more time spent in the surf, larger waves, more wipe-outs, long swims, fights for survival against the sea, and possibly contact with hazardous marine life. The knowledge and skills that make surfing safer and more enjoyable are called *surfmanship*. The better a surfer knows the ocean and the nature of waves, the safer he will be.

Any accident in the water can lead to drowning, which claims thousands of lives each year. Swimming, boating, skin diving, water skiing, and surfing accidents are almost always preventable. The extra person overloading the boat, the novice skin diver with his first scuba, the poor swimmer trying to make it across the lake, and the fledgling surfer riding a wipe-out wave all chance drowning because they lack experience and skill. Safety in water sports boils down to following these basic guides:

Become a strong swimmer.
Know your limitations and abilities

Understand the hazards of your sport.

Learn the dangers of the particular area in which you surf, swim, sail, dive, etc.

Know your equipment and its limitations.

Learn and practice rescue skills, first aid, and artificial respiration techniques.

Use the "buddy system." A partner adds safety as well as companionship.

Drownings are preventable. They don't just happen. A drowning is a culmination of a chain of events that begins when someone is careless, or knowingly takes an unreasonable chance with his or someone else's life. Plan ahead: a few minutes of wave watching, current guessing, and weather predicting make water sports safer. Avoid critical situations where violent collisions are possible, where waves can't be ridden safely, and where rocks and currents create unavoidable hazards.

Surfing accidents usually are caused by collision with another board, or rocks, or by a blasting wipe-out in the shorebreak. Many accidents occur when a board pearls, shoots up in the air, and comes down on its owner or another surfer. These can be prevented with good board control. Experts develop great ability to direct their boards to exactly the right spot at the right time. Board control means the skill to cut out of a wave quickly, turn back, stall, and make a successful pullout. These basic skills should be learned as soon as possible. Too many novices slide a wave with no idea of how to guide their board or avoid a wipe-out. Many surfing accidents are violent split-second incidents that end with missing teeth and sutures crisscrossing the scalp. *Protect yourself at all times* is a watchword of surfing. Or as the old wooden-ship sailors used to say, "One hand for the ship and one for yourself." In this case, one hand hangs on to the board and the other curls over your head as protection from a skeg zipping past.

The wipe-out. Note the nose of the surfboard just under the water. This is *pearling*.

Wipe-outs

Surfers talk endlessly about wipe-outs. Wipe-outs are as much a part of surfing as the waves themselves. They happen over and over again. The severity of a wipe-out depends on several factors. Wipe-outs in deep water with no rocks below are not as dangerous as a ride over the falls in the shore-break. The little wipe-outs in shallow water with other boards and surfers close by present as awful a danger as being smothered by a large wave.

Most beginners have no idea of the correct procedure for handling a wipe-out safely. The first rule of course, is to avoid a wipe-out if at all possible. These spills can mean long swims, being caught in a rip current, and possibly being hit by your own board. The simple way to avoid a wipe-out is to kick out of the wave. Stay alert, anticipate what the wave is going to do, and judge the right time to pull out. It's quite natural to try to stay in the wave as long as possible, but there is the split second when it's either kick out or get blasted off the board. Probably two-thirds of all wipe-outs result from staying with the wave too long. Surfers seem to be part gambler and like to press the odds of staying on the wave to the limit, but this is like playing against the house; you're bound to lose most of the time.

It's easy to recognize a wipe-out situation. The wave will crest suddenly and a great amount of whiteness will begin to tower over or around you. If you try to ride the wave too close to shore it will suddenly collapse around you and rush up the beach with board and body all rolling around together. Another kind of wipe-out starts as the wave begins to break in front of you. This is a sure indication that it's time to kick out or take a spill.

If the wipe-out can't be prevented it can sometimes be controlled. If a wipe-out is coming and you can't kick out it's sometimes possible to turn the board toward shore and ride the white water lying prone. An expert surfer can cut shoreward, remain standing, and ride the soup in. Beginners will have better luck controlling the board by dropping to the knees and then the stomach and riding in this way. When riding prone the weight should be shifted quite far back to keep the nose of the board up and prevent pearling. *Proning in* is a good technique to use because the surfer retains control of the board, avoids a swim or walk over the rocks, and knows he won't get hit by his board. Practice riding prone once in a while; the skill will come in handy time and time again.

If the wipe-out is quick and critical and you know the board is going to be ripped from your grasp, try to keep away from it. Remember, a board that noses in with great velocity is going to come up again, and sometimes it flies many feet in the air. If you know your board has pearled sufficiently to be sent flying, then play frogman and dive deep—the deeper the better. Stay underwater until you're sure the wave and flying board have passed by. If you're falling, try to avoid landing on the shore side of the board. This eliminates the possibility of the board washing into you. In shorebreak surf where the water is shallow this is particularly important.

Wipe-outs in big surf present a double danger. The first is being hit by the board and the second is the tremendous force of water that will pound and surround you. Big-wave surfers tell stories about being driven many feet deep by a giant collapsing wave and being held under a minute or more. These are exaggerations but fifteen seconds underwater with the wind knocked out of you and the water churning around and around seem like two or three minutes. These situations call for calm, deliberate action. Panic only makes a tight situation worse. Before taking the journey over the falls grab a big breath and go under with the lungs full. Once underwater, relax and keep heading toward the bottom. The water between you and the crushing wave above will help cushion the shock. A violent struggle only uses up precious oxygen. With the body relaxed, you can remain below until the water above has calmed somewhat. If you lose your orientation underwater during the somersaulting, churning wipe-out, use the light filtering through the water as the direction in which to swim. This kind of wipe-out is rare, but if you're ever involved in one, remember that light means up and oxygen, dark means the bottom.

A wipe-out in shallow water is especially dangerous if the bottom is rocky or a coral reef lies below. Try to land with your body flat on the surface of the water. This prevents the body from diving and smashing on the rocks. After the wipe-out remember to look around when coming up. A survey of the water may reveal loose boards, surfers riding toward you or another giant wave to dive under. Always get a breath of air immediately upon surfacing—it might be the last for another half minute.

A safety technique that seems instinctive is protecting the

head. Self-preservation dictates that the arms be wrapped around the head when there is danger of falling objects, and there are plenty of falling objects on a crowded wave with boards flying through the air in all directions at the same time. If you can hold on to your board after a wipe-out, use it as a protective shield against oncoming boards. A sharp fiberglass skeg passing overhead at twenty-five miles an hour can cut a good slice through flesh and bone.

Rip Currents and Wild Water

Rip currents and rough water cause most emergencies at the beach. On a hard-driving surf day along crowded beaches in Hawaii or Southern California rip rescues may mount to several hundred. Off Zuma Beach, California, a giant fast-moving rip sucked twenty-eight bathers out for several hundred yards. Conditions were so hazardous in the crashing waves at the shoreline that the guards couldn't bring the bathers to shore. They had to call the rescue boat, load the victims aboard and deposit them miles away at a pier. Sunset Beach, Hawaii, is perhaps the king of rip makers. Several years ago seven servicemen were caught in an extremely bad rip and carried rapidly seaward. Before rescue attempts could be made all of the men drowned. An inexperienced surfer was caught in a Sunset Beach rip and couldn't make it back on his own; one of the great all-time surfers, Buzzy Trent, was flown out by helicopter to save him. Buzzy and board dropped into the water and guided the unfortunate surfer back safely to the beach.

Rip currents are caused by massive amounts of seawater piling up in shallow areas near the beach. This water must find a way to flow back and seek its natural level. In the process it rushes seaward along the easiest path it can find. Strong currents are thus created which will run out to sea swiftly. Two opposing currents can also create a rip. If currents meet along the shore they will conflict and tend to move seaward until their individual energies are expended.

Rip currents can be recognized by several signs. Since these currents are running along or offshore with some speed they pick up sand and hold it in suspension. The sand gives the water a slightly off-color appearance. This indicates that a rip is present. A strong rip is usually characterized by a triangle of lighter-colored water or of foam pointing out to sea. Most rips are not very wide, perhaps twenty yards at the most, although some are wider. Even a strong swimmer will have trouble moving against these currents. The general rule is not to fight the current, but to float with it until it diminishes. Sometimes you can move out of a rip by swimming diagonally across the current, like swimming across a fast river. Rips are sometimes used by surfers as an aquatic tramway to take them seaward. Some rips are so strong that it's impossible to paddle against them. They often move at speeds of five miles an hour. The best course for a surfer is to avoid a rip. Learn to recognize rip conditions. At unfamiliar beaches ask the locals or lifeguards about hazards.

Judging Waves

Judging where, when and how waves will break is an important part of surfing. Knowing with a fair degree of certainty how a wave will form, crest, and roll shoreward gives you a basis for planning your ride and enjoying it in confidence and safety.

The form of a wave before it becomes a breaker determines whether it can be ridden, how far the ride will go, and the possibilities of a wipe-out. From the beach you can get a general indication of which way the swell is running and if ridable shoulders are being formed. A wave that dumps over and crashes along its entire length just cannot be ridden—unless it is a gradual spiller and you want to ride the white water. Look for a wave that has one side or the other holding. Perhaps the swell is marginal and only one or two waves out of a set can be ridden. If you recognize these in advance you'll have a ride. Look for swells that have one

An almost perfect *set* at Rincon, California. All three surfers are in different positions reacting individually to their own waves. The back wave is the largest and is called an *overhead* wave.

side lower than the other. The lower portions break later due to the wave-height-water-depth relationship. From the viewpoint of the surfer in the water an individual wave can be judged a little better. Suppose the wave looks good, the surfer decides to try for it and makes his start and turn. As he rides he'll be able to notice if the wave is peaking up in front to the extent that it will spill over and break in front of him. If the wave is about to break it's time either to pull out or prone-ride shoreward. Most wipe-outs happen because the surfer stays in the wave too long and doesn't pull out in time. Each wave is different and the surfer on his board must make a decision based on a quick survey of the wave. Watch carefully and learn the signs of the surf.

The person sitting on a board waiting for a ride or the person just about to launch and paddle out can look toward the horizon and see sets of waves coming long before they arrive if the day is clear and the visibility good. A slight rising of the horizon in an uneven line indicates swells are coming. Before a swell arrives the surface of the water toward the horizon will be flat if the wind isn't blowing hard. As a set approaches, the level of the water will appear to rise. It is sometimes possible to determine which wave will be the largest by taking a close look into the distance. The experienced wave watcher can then pick his wave and position his board accordingly. Some surfers stand on their boards to see farther. The person paddling out can see a little farther on the top of a swell. If the waves are big the incoming swell will lift the board and rider several feet or more in the air. Before the board settles back down in the trough take a fast look and see what is coming. For beginners it is better to take the last wave of the set to avoid getting caught inside when the next big wave comes.

Marine Life Hazards

Sharks. Surfers, swimmers, and skin divers consider sharks the most dangerous of marine animal-life hazards.

Sharks are commonest off Australia, but attacks occur all over the world and in almost every body of water the sea reaches. Sharks have attacked people in rivers where the tide runs, off heavily attended public beaches, and in open water miles from land. Of the 250 or so species only 25 or 30 are considered dangerous. Most sharks found off surfing beaches are not the killer variety, but local inhabitants who go about their business of devouring smaller fish instead of swimmers and surfers.

Most of the verified shark attacks have occurred off Australian beaches—over 200 recorded attacks in the past 150 years. Australians have gone to great efforts to protect their swimmers: Shark patrols, nets strung along beaches, and watchtowers for early warning of approaching sharks. Every year about a dozen shark attacks are reported worldwide. Each report draws wide attention. People become shark conscious for awhile and then tend to forget until the next incident.

The shark is a predator, a sort of seagoing wolf or lion. The shark's eating habits are indiscriminate and he will gobble up almost anything containing food value. These facts may be useful to surfers:

Sharks depend as much on their sense of smell for obtaining food as on their sight. Blood attracts sharks far beyond their range of visibility.

Both living and dead food matter attracts.

Sharks can attack from any angle. They do not have to roll over on their sides or back to bite.

There is no single tactic used by sharks when attacking. Some attacks are leisurely and deliberate; others occur with lightening-fast speed.

There is no absolutely safe shark repellent. Colored dye repellents may cloud the water and obscure the swimmer from the shark, but no type of repellent has been proved totally effective to date.

The one general rule to follow when sighting a dorsal fin cutting across the water is to leave the area quickly and with as little panic as possible. Thrashing the water will only betray your location. Paddle smoothly and quietly toward shallow water. Although sharks normally avoid shallow water, enough attacks have occurred there to negate a hard and fast rule. (The author was followed by a shark once into three feet of water, at which point he could walk across the water to dry sand.) The surfboard itself offers some protection. And common sense suggests that a legs-up position on the board is advisable.

Sea Urchins. Sea urchins are frequently found in great profusion in tropic waters. The sea urchin (called *vana* in Hawaii) looks like a fat purple or black pincushion with very long needles sticking point upward. These spines discourage other marine creatures from feasting on the sea urchin. The surfer falling or walking on a sea urchin will take away a souvenir of spines imbedded in his flesh.

Sea urchins are quite abundant in shallow waters. The long brittle spines are often a hazard to falling surfers.

Ron Church

Sea urchins usually collect together in rocky areas known as sea urchin beds. When falling over known or suspected concentrations of sea urchins try to land flat so the body will not sink into contact with the spines. If you have to swim over urchins, use the breast stroke and keep as much of the body parallel to the surface as possible.

If you're unlucky and return to shore with spines under your skin, pull them out carefully without breaking the spines. If portions remain under the skin they can cause infection. Soak the spine-infected limb as soon as possible in a solution of hot water and epsom salts. This aids removal and eases pain. If the spines cannot be readily removed, consult a doctor.

Coral. Countless years go into building a coral reef. The animal which forms a coral reef is called a *polyp*. As the polyp starts its life cycle it builds a tiny limestone platform between its body and a rock or other coral. Next the polyp builds an outside skeleton of lime leaving only its mouth and feelers exposed to feed on passing organisms. Vast colonies of polyps reproduce at such a terrific rate that reefs and islands are built from their skeletal remains. Coral reefs are abundant in southern Florida, Hawaii, and in most tropic waters.

A collision with the sharp surfaces of coral produces deep lacerations which permit the entrance of microscopic bacteria. Coral poisoning, a serious infection, can result. Cuts from coral should be treated immediately. Wash with a mild soap and apply an antiseptic. Consult a doctor if infection starts.

Cold Water and Fatigue

When the water temperature drops into the low sixties or below and the wind blows, the surfer sitting on a wet board with wet hair, skin, and trunks loses body heat very rapidly. Muscles become tense and stiff, the body starts shaking, hands and feet grow numb. Fine control of the board, so

Feet forward and parallel, body crouched under the curling crest—this is fast, exciting surfing at its best. It's winter and both surfers wear *wet suits*—Malibu Beach.

necessary for safety, is no longer possible. Either avoid cold water or get a *wet suit* surfing or skin-diving shirt.

The foam neoprene skin diver's jacket has been adapted and used by surfers for several years. Acting as insulation, the jacket prevents the upper torso from losing heat. Unless the water is in the fifties or colder the top alone is sufficient; in very cold water use the neoprene trousers as well. The surfer's jacket is usually cut slightly fuller than the diver's shirt because the arms need freedom for paddling. The wet suit jacket material is buoyant and acts as a life preserver. A surfing wet suit top costs from $10 to $15 and up. The extra comfort and safety are really worth the cost.

Surfing Rules of the Road

With thousands of newcomers, surfing needs its own code of conduct. Most surfers agree on the following points:

Surf at your own level of skill. Take a wave only if your skill is adequate to the demands of the particular wave. A novice surfer mixed up with several experts on a fast-moving wave can cause a mass wipe-out. As the surfer's level of ability improves he'll be accepted on better waves.

Allow the expert the advantage if several persons are taking off on the same wave. He knows how to avoid collisions and can cut and turn to help others on the same wave.

Avoid riding toward surfers paddling out. The surfer on a wave has more control than the paddler or swimmer and it's his responsibility to avoid the paddler. When riding in, anticipate having to cut and turn away from others. If avoiding a collision means losing the wave by all means drop out of it. There are always other waves.

Avoid areas where there are bathers or swimmers. Young children don't realize the danger of a surfboard rushing up the shore. They will often run to grab the board and be hit by it. When surfing at a public beach check with the lifeguards about local rules and regulations. At some beaches surfers are permitted to ride until about midmorning or when swimmers begin to congregate. The split-day method works quite well; both surfers and swimmers benefit.

Don't force another surfer to drop out of a wave. If the wave is crowded the man in front or the farthest ahead of the break should avoid cutting back into other surfers. He should also stay far enough in front of the break so that surfers closer to the white water will be able to stay out of the soup and continue in the wave.

Don't take off directly in front of another rider. A surfer sliding a fast wall might not be able to cut back and then let the person taking off get started and turn. Any collision course tactic should be avoided.

Paddlers going out should work their way around the direct route of incoming surfers. Paddlers also have a responsibility to avoid collisions. It's a bit scary to be paddling out and face fifteen or more boards bearing down at you on a large fast-moving wave. One fall in this kind of jammed-up wave will escalate and in a second or two half the riders and their boards will be washing over and around the paddler.

Keep your board in good repair. Loose flaps of fiberglass, rough rails and jagged edges on the skeg can cut and tear the skin. Sharp edges of fiberglass should be torn off until the board can be repaired. Old fiberglass begins to slough off in minute amounts after several years. Sometimes this glass gets under the skin, causing very annoying itching. A fresh coat of resin (called a gloss coat) will prevent this and make the board slide better.

Don't lose control of the board. This is a number one safety rule. If the board is always kept thoroughly waxed the chances of slipping are less and control is better.

And last, *surf with a* heads-up *attitude.* Be aware of what's happening to the wave you're riding. Know where other surfers are and use the eyes to tell you of hazards and anything that will affect your safety on the ride in and the paddle out.

Chapter 6

INTERMEDIATE SURFING SKILLS

AFTER a few surfing trips, and the experience of really riding a wave, the new surfer gets the bug to start sliding larger and more difficult surf. Intermediate surfing skills are required for stand-up surfing, the fast takeoff, advanced turns and pullouts, bigger and better wipe-outs and the never-ending problems of surf safety. With these skills you graduate from small waves to surf five and six feet high. These larger waves are sometimes called *overhead* surf because the waves will be over the head of a man if he's riding in the trough. When surfers say the surf is breaking overhead, and holding, it's time to grab a surfboard and head for the beach. Surf this high is not the rule but the hope of most mainland surfers. Surf of five and six feet is ideal for most styles and techniques of surfing practiced today.

The goal at this point in a person's surfing career will be to learn to ride a wave safely with others, handle a critical wipe-out and compete for his share of the surf. Mastering intermediate skills will allow the beginner to graduate to the ultimate surfing experience—the fast controlled ride across the face on an unbroken wave. Control is stressed here, because with control the surfer can begin to perform and use the moving wall of water to give his ride purpose. Control on a wave means the ability to turn, to cut back and to use

77

the riding forward position. Riding forward is a term used here to cover all sorts of nose-riding styles like *hanging five* and ten toes over, head dips, and others. There is almost endless variety to the stunts and styles possible on a surfboard, but there is also a responsibility to master control before becoming a fancy footwork expert. Here, then, are the skills that lead to control over board and wave.

The Takeoff

The takeoff (start) and the turn that follows help determine how well the remainder of the ride will go. If the start is late the chances for a wipe-out are good; if too early, the wave might not get picked up at all.

Let's pull Barney, our fictitious surfer, off the beach again and send him out to slide a set of five- or six-foot-high waves. Barney has waxed his board carefully and paddled out with a few other surfers. On the way out he watches for incoming riders and loose boards. He's still a little unsure of his ability and sits slightly to one side of the main group. He has been watching the surf from the beach and has a good idea of where he wants to wait for his takeoff. Barney must decide several things before committing himself to a wave. First, and most important, he sizes up the hazards that await him on the ride in: how many other surfers will he have to share the wave with; what about reefs or rocks sticking up underwater; and what will the shorebreak be like? Before starting he also checks for other surfers paddling out or taking off on either side. Next, Barney judges how the waves are holding and if a consistent shoulder is being formed. He should be able to tell if the wave is a crasher and will close out on him during the ride in. A *close-out* is when the wave curls over and crashes in front or over the rider before he finishes the ride. Barney is lucky this day. The surf is well formed and the wave faces are broad and steep enough to support several surfers riding together. Barney waits on the outside of the group, the farthest one from where the wave will start breaking. He wants to ride, but he doesn't want to get mixed up in a mass wipe-out yet.

The wave comes and Barney begins to paddle. He doesn't start too soon, but begins paddling just before the wave peaks up in back of him. He digs in hard to attain maximum speed for the takeoff. The tail of his board lifts, and Barney feels the excitement of the slide starting.

What are the problems of the start and riding medium to large surf? On a small to medium-sized wave (two to five feet), starting the slide can be done closer to the top of the wave than on a larger wave. This is because the board is tipped to a sliding angle sooner. On a larger wave, the board must be paddled farther down the front slope of the wave before the slide and ride start.

Sometimes you won't be in just the right position for a takeoff. If you are inside the break and white water is coming all around you, there's not much defense except to turn turtle or head into the breaker and bust through. Another method to keep from being washed inshore or apart from the board is to sit on the tail end and sink the rear of the board. This makes the board and rider more resistant to the shock of the white water and acts somewhat like a sea anchor. Don't forget to hold on tightly.

Turning

Usually the turn away from the break is started the moment the surfer comes to his feet. (The exception to this rule is the slow lazy wave that can be ridden almost straight off, like the surf at Waikiki and San Onofre. A board turns because of the drag or friction being applied to one side or the other. This causes one edge of the board to slide faster. This drag is produced by downward pressure of the rear foot. The more the downward push, the more friction and the faster the board will turn.

Barney has had a chance to practice now. Let's see how he's doing standing up, taking off and turning. On the next

wave as Barney changes from a paddling position to a standing position, his hands move to the board in front of his
body. As he comes to his feet, his arms help push him up
and maintain balance. In one smooth motion he rises to his
feet. This part of the start can be practiced on dry land and
right on top of the board. Place the board on the sand or
ground with the skeg set so the board doesn't tip. Coming
to the feet from the knees or prone position should both be
practiced. Moving from the kneeling position to the standing
position is a whole body motion. At the end of the final
paddling stroke, the hands are placed in front of the body
to help in the rise to the feet. As the board begins to slide
the surfer pushes with his arms and rises to his feet. Since
the board is heading downward, the hands also help maintain balance. The whole motion is quite natural and with a
little dry-land practice standing comes quickly. Coming to
the feet from the prone position is almost the same. Most
surfers come directly to the feet and bypass the intermediate
kneeling position. Coming to the feet from lying prone
should be done as one smooth fluid motion. As the surfer
comes to his feet, the right foot goes back and the left foot
forward. As the rear foot moves back, it is turned almost to
a right angle from the center line of the board. The front
foot is at about a 45° angle from the center line. The feet are
about a foot and a half to two feet apart, depending on the
size of the surfer. The legs are bent slightly at the knees and
the upper torso leans forward. The legs are flexed and the
whole body is balanced so a rapid shift of weight can be
made forward or backward.

Returning to Barney and his start: After making the start
and coming to his feet he begins the standing turn. To turn,
Barney shifts his weight to his rear foot, leans slightly in the
direction he wants to go and the board begins to turn away
from the break. From behind Barney a surfer races toward
him calling "Cut! Cut!" which means, "Watch out, I'm coming through and need room!" With a board crowding close

on his tail Barney knows he'd better cut fast. He shifts his weight even farther back and to the inside rail (the edge cutting through the wave) and his board responds. Now the board is turned away from the break and begins to race on. Barney shifts the weight to his forward foot, drops the nose of the board and brings it into trim. The board picks up

Perfect balance. The surfer has his left foot forward, his right foot back and at right angles to the center line of the board. The weight is carried over the middle of the board and he can react to sudden changes of balance quickly.

Dick Gustafson

speed and he moves away from the rider on his tail. He avoided a possible collision and is sliding straight and fast.

There are several variations of turning, but the two basic types to learn first are the foot-to-the-rear turn and the leaning turn. The foot-to-the-rear turn is done by moving the back foot near the inside rail of the board and shifting the weight on it. This is a good turn to learn and practice because both feet remain firmly planted on the board and better balance is achieved. With the rear foot back and turning almost at right angles to the length of the board, the downward pressure increases the drag on the inside rail and the board begins to turn. The rear foot turn is good to use after the takeoff because it allows a faster and better balanced turn. One point to consider in making any turn is that the forward rail must be far enough out of the water so it doesn't dig in. The more pressure applied to the tail of the board during the turn the more it will respond. If the downward push is sufficiently hard and prolonged, the board will either pull out of the wave or stall, and the wave will pass the surfer by.

The second basic turn is the leaning turn. The leaning turn is slower and more rhythmic. It is a little harder to master than the foot-to-the-rear turn, but it is graceful and very useful for cutting back into the break. In the leaning turn the feet are placed in the usual standing riding position with the forward toes pointing about 45° from the center line of the board. To make the turn, the weight is simply shifted toward the rail on the side toward which you want to turn. The leaning turn must be done at a fast speed to overcome the pull of gravity when the body moves outward from the balance point of the surfboard. The upper body may even lean beyond the rails and over the water. The arms and the speed of the board are used in this turn to counterbalance the leaning body movements. When leaning back on the heels, the arms are raised in front of the body; when leaning forward, the arms go back. Of course the

With a kick and a push on the rear of the board the surfer swings his board away from the break. In a moment when he's beyond the break, he'll walk forward, drop the nose, and bring the board into trim.

The leaning turn. The surfer has dropped down the face of the wave after the start, shifted his weight back and leans in the direction of the turn.

Dick Gustafson

A bottom turn. The surfer has dropped down the front of this medium-size wave, is in a slightly stalling position prior to cutting away.

amount of lean to give depends on the individual's body size, the speed he is riding, and the condition of the surf.

In the past ten years design changes in surfboards have influenced the styles of turns made by surfers. The broad-tailed Malibu-type board spins or pivots much faster than the older and longer planks. Because of this fast maneuverability, turning has become an art. On larger waves, these fast-turning boards have a tendency to spin out due to their lack of stability at higher speeds. Because of this, the turn is made closer to the bottom of the wave and the chances of a wipe-out are greater. To overcome this problem, surfers have developed what is called the bottom turn.

The development of the bottom turn has captivated the surfing world. The bottom turn has become a fad, and like most fads this turn has become the thing to do. The bottom turn is a useful maneuver, and sometimes necessary, but it is only one facet of turning and shouldn't be used to the exclusion of others. The bottom turn can be made at any spot below the crest of a wave where the height is sufficient for a sweeping type of turn, though it is most often made at the bottom lower front of the wave. This turn starts right after the takeoff. Instead of cutting away from the break and racing across the face of the wave, the surfer holds his starting slide and drops rapidly down the face of the wave. This allows the board to gain great speed. When the board reaches the almost flat portion in front of the wave the surfer makes an aggressive leaning or bank-type turn away from the break. The speed gained during the descent from the top of the wave helps the rider cut sharply back and up the wave toward the crest. Before the board loses speed and begins to stall, it is brought back into trim and the rider can race away from the white water. The bottom turn probably evolved at big-surf beaches, like Sunset in Hawaii. At Sunset Beach, for example, the face of the waves near the crest is so rough, steep and choppy from the effects of offshore winds that a turn near the top often results in the rider being blown over the top of the wave or bounced from the board. The fall from the top of a Sunset wave to the trough isn't the most pleasant surfing experience. Also, if the top portion of the wave is sufficiently steep there just isn't enough water for the skeg and the tail of the board to dig into and the board will side slip and spin out.

During the drop to the wave trough, the surfer's weight is kept back toward the tail to prevent pearling. This helps keep the nose up and the tail dug in the wave, which makes a rapid bank turn easier. When the bottom turn is made, the rear foot drives down on the tail aggressively and swings the board about. This all happens at high speed and in a quick fluid motion. As the turn begins, the body rotates slightly ahead of the foot action. It often appears that the rider is completely off balance. It only looks this way because the board is tipped but the rider is still directly in line with the center of the board. This leaning effect is like the high-speed bicycle or motorcycle rider taking a sharp turn.

The kickout, first phase. Here the surfer has stalled the board, forced it down with a hard shift of weight to the rear foot, and is beginning to swing the nose up and over the wave.

The kickout, second phase. The tail of the board is forced down and the nose of the board is on its way over the top of the wave. At this point the board has almost stopped forward motion.

Perhaps the hardest to master is the kick turn. This is the fastest turn and requires the most body movement. The kick turn is a variation of the foot-to-the-rear turn, but with added body rotation and rear foot emphasis. The turn is started by placing the rear foot closer to the tail and stomping down quite heavily. This sinks the tail of the board and points the nose up. As this is going on, the surfer rotates his body in the direction of the turn. This upper body rotation helps swing the board around. If the turn and position are held, the turn becomes a pullout. To recover from the kick turn and continue the ride, the weight must be shifted toward the nose again and the board brought into trim. The weight can be directed forward either by leaning or stepping toward the nose.

The turns discussed here can be used in various combinations. The intermediate surfer should practice all of them.

This is trim. The rider is in balance, the board is stable, and the rider is in control. The board is kept close to the break and the surfer can move toward the nose with the wave holding the tail down.

Dick Gustafson

He should also be able to use these turns sliding either right or left.

Once the ride begins, and the surfer is really in the wave, it is again time to use judgment. The new surfer must consider what is happening to the wave he is on, what the other surfers are doing, and what he must do with the board. After the takeoff and the turn, the rider must stabilize the board and bring it into trim.

Trim

Trimming the surfboard to slide efficiently becomes more and more important in medium to large surf. If a board is properly trimmed for the individual wave, more speed can be obtained, better balance achieved and there will be less chance for a wipe-out. On fast-breaking waves, good trim can mean the difference between having the wave close out over the surfer or being able to outrace the break. Each board will come into trim with slight individual differences. Shorter boards require more attention to bring into trim than do larger, more stable big-wave boards. Trim on a slow lazy wave means riding almost straight off to stay in the steep portion of the wave. If the board is trimmed improperly in this type of surf, the rider will fall away from the breaking portion and stall out. On a rapidly breaking wave with a fast-collapsing shoulder, the surfer must trim for maximum speed in order to keep in front of the break. In this type of wave, the board's nose is dropped as far as possible without pearling and the weight of the surfer is carried forward. Often surfers will crouch on a fast wave to make themselves streamlined and reduce air resistance. On a wave where a tunnel or tube is being formed as the crest spills over, the surfer must crouch in order to fit in the tube or else get wiped out by the falling water. *Shooting the tube* is one of the most exciting tricks that can be performed on a medium to large size wave. The surfer rides in such a position that the wave actually curls and falls over him, but not on him. If the board is in trim and the surfer under control, he can remain in the tube for several seconds or longer and then race for open water again. A ride in the tube is a memorable experience. Few surfers ever forget the feeling of being completely surrounded by water and the dimming of light from the wave curling overhead. Good trim and control make it possible to shoot the tube.

Walking the Board

Being able to change the balance of the board by quickly walking forward or backward is an important surfing skill. On-the-nose surfing is possible only when the rider can move forward and then return to a stable position near the center of the board. Walking is also important because sometimes a lean forward and backward just won't make the board respond fast enough. The simplest way to walk the board is to shuffle forward. The other way is to actually walk by placing one foot in front of the other. The shuffle should be learned first because it is easier and both feet are always in contact with the top deck of the board. The shuffle is done by simply moving the forward foot ahead and then moving the rear foot after it. This is the basic, natural way to move on the board, though walking is faster and more graceful.

The intermediate surfer will have to practice both shuffling and walking many times before it comes naturally. A good way to get the idea of the foot movement is to walk on the deck of the board on dry sand. What makes walking hard is that one foot, the rear one, must cross in front of the forward foot. Then the forward foot is moved and it is again leading. This walking forward or back is almost like a simple dance step.

Once the walk is mastered, the surfer is ready to think about doing some beginning hot-dogging. *Hot-dogging* or fancy surfing falls into a category which is best described as riding forward. Riding forward includes such styles as nose riding, toes over and hanging five or ten.

The forward riding style gives a feeling of great speed. It's almost as if there were no board under you. Some surfers claim nothing else gives them such a feeling of oneness with the wave. This style is a bit show-offish, but it's a good way to demonstrate ability. Riding forward also adds to the excitement because it makes wipe-outs more risky. The hardest forward riding style is hanging ten. To get the toes over the nose rails, the board must be supported by fast surf that keeps it planing. When the body is this far forward, balance is hard to hold and the wave can't be ridden very far. The board has to be very much in the break because the tail is held down by the breaking portion of the wave. In the next chapter, the various styles of riding forward are covered in more detail.

Turning While Riding

Often a surfer needs to slow the board or he will ride too far from the breaking portion of the wave and lose his ride. The *stall* is a modification of the pullout. It is done by moving the balance toward the tail of the board. This creates drag and the board slows until it is brought back into trim. Another way of producing a stall is to *cut back* into the wave by using a lean or foot-to-the-rear turn.

From the stall, the surfer can either pull out of the wave, cut back to the curl, or turn away from the break and slide again. The turn into the wave, or cutback, is an exciting maneuver.

On most waves the rider picks up more speed than the wave and soon rides beyond the break and finds himself without sufficient slope to slide on. Here's where the cutback comes in handy. A fast cutback will turn the rider back toward the breaking portion of the wave and permit him to pick up the wave again. To make a successful cutback, the surfer should be in a good trimmed position to start with. His board should be somewhere slightly higher than midpoint on the wave. If the board is too low it will lose speed during the turn, stall out, or be caught by the charging curl. If the board is held too high on the wave when the turn is started, the outside rail will dig in as the board is turned toward the break. The actual turn is made by both a lean and body swing in the direction of the turn. This arm swing is somewhat like the body rotation skiers use while turning. As in most athletics, the surfer should look in the direction he is going to turn. This is like the baseball coach saying "Keep your eyes on the ball!"

Once the cutback is made and the surfer faces the spilling white water of the break, he can either make a bottom turn or a standard turn away from the curl. Cutting back and forth should be done with a smooth fluid motion. Movement should be continuous throughout the turns. Continuous movement keeps up speed and gives the surfer the necessary velocity to sweep in and out of the turns. If a stall comes during the turn there may not be time to climb back up on the face of the wave, build up speed and race away from the break.

On some waves that are just a little fast to cut back into and just slow enough to race ahead on, the surfer can check his speed and stay close to the break by climbing and dropping. A board can be made to climb and drop by edging the inside rail into the wave. This is done by leaning into the wave. The lean drops the rail, creates drag and the board climbs. Dropping, which will speed the slide, is done by leaning away from the wave. This lessens the friction on the inside rail and allows the board to sideslip down the wave front. The drop and climb can be done with a rhythmic swing of the body that is quite pleasing. Alternating climbs and drops reduces speed without losing control and without taking the chance of a wipe-out on a cutback.

Surfing With Others

The critical test for the surfer is the ability to ride safely on the same wave with others. Surfing has become a mass-participation sport and sharing a wave is part of the game. Riding with others can be fun, especially if the people on the same wave know what they're doing, have a good sense of sportsmanship and consider the other surfer. On a crowded wave, a certain amount of give and take is necessary to prevent mass wipe-outs and injuries. Some waves just won't support more than one or two surfers, but big lazy smooth-fronted combers can handle several dozen surfers all mushing shoreward together. Don't start off with fifteen or twenty or even five others if the face of the wave won't support this many. The size of the wave and the speed at which it is breaking are the relevant factors here.

The surfer who picks up the wave first, usually from far outside, has the right-of-way. People trying for the same wave, but from a point closer to shore, have to consider that the surfer already in the wave will be coming in fast. He may not be able to cut away from the person taking off. Beginning surfers usually are forced to ride the portion of the wave that is furthest from the break. When they start to take off there may be several others on the same wave already standing in trim. Taking off in front of a group like this usually means a collision or a near miss. The last person to take off on a wave should make sure he's not going to get in the way. Once in the wave with others, it's important to keep track of how long the wave is going to hold before breaking. If the wave collapses over several people, there's going to be a big tangle of boards and bodies and chances are someone will get bruised. The best course is to pull out of the wave before it breaks. If the surfers are all jumbled up together, it's harder to pull out. A kick turn will whip the nose of the board around and clip another surfer across the ankles or the knees. The answer: Stall the board and let the rest of the pack ride on. The surfer on the outside of the break, the one farthest from the white water, should keep as far as possible in front of the wave to let others have room to ride and maneuver. The person in front spot will also have the best chance to make a safe pullout if the wave should collapse suddenly. If the wave is high enough and holding well, it is possible for surfers to pass in front of each other. This kind of teamwork can make riding a wave with another truly enjoyable. The surfer traveling fastest passes in front of the slower-riding person. Usually the slower person is at the bottom or the very top of the wave and the surfer overtaking him is trimmed for maximum speed and is riding near the crest. The surfer being passed should maneuver his board so the other rider can pass as free from a collision course as possible. The riders can then change positions and start an artistic weaving pattern on the same wave face. One caution here, though—the rider nearest the top of the wave should be careful not to get wiped out while directly over the person passing underneath, for obvious reasons.

Surfing with others is heads-up surfing—on a crowded wave there is no place for daydreaming. It takes teamwork coupled with skill to ride crowded waves. Beginners should avoid the many boarded wave and develop skill until he or she is ready to join the pack.

Chapter 7

HOT-DOGGING

ACROSS the face of a fast-breaking wave someone appears to be surfing on the balls of his feet. A second, more careful look reveals that the surfer is so far forward on the nose of the board that his toes are curled over the edge. This is the modern surfing style known as hot-dogging. The surfer in question was hanging ten toes over the nose of the board, demonstrating his ability to friends on the beach.

Hot-dogging is a recent addition to the old game of surfing. The riders of last generation's giant redwood surfboards couldn't do much with their boards except paddle for a swell and share its power and speed until the ride ended. Today's surfer has developed a style to match the new lightweight board. At first hot-dogging was practiced by a very few surfers at beaches where the surf was small to medium size and steep enough to make fast cuts and turns possible. But today the advanced style has become so popular that surfers ride forward and on the nose even on the big heavyweight waves of Hawaii.

As the sport's popularity mushroomed and the better surfing beaches became crowded, surfers resorted to lesser beaches and unpredictable waves. These called for fast execution of each maneuver. Thus the development of hot-dogging. On-the-nose surfing in small waves and in the shorebreak is a game of fast reflexes and acrobatic movements. Surfing under these conditions permits no time for judgment; it is either make the right move, or get blasted off the board. On the brief fast forward rides, surfers have developed all sorts of stunts and surfing gymnastics. New words describing the tricks have entered the surfer's lexicon—quasimodo, head dips, el spontanio and mysterioso all became part of surfing patois. Though some hot-dogging tricks are not functional, they display the rider's skill and ability to master the wave for one brief moment. Nose riding provides a unique thrill that perhaps accounts for its popularity—when the surfer is completely forward it's almost like surfing without a board.

Hot-dogging played an important role in boosting surfing to the level of national interest. Hot-doggers developed individual styles that identified them to their friends on the beach. They became known for their riding stunts and their fame spread from beach to beach. Soon there was a surfing personality cult. Younger surfers spoke of their heroes and looked for their pictures in surfing magazines. As top surfers generated individual followings, enterprising businessmen invited them to endorse surf products such as boards and swimming trunks. This was the sure sign that surfing had come of age: it was being commercialized.

Learning the riding forward style requires a solid background of basic surfing techniques. Such maneuvers as the pullout, kickout, and cutback are necessary for riding the nose. In addition, a special type of wave is required. On-the-nose surf should be smooth, almost glassy, and of small to medium height. The hot-dogging wave should peak up to a sharp wall and have a fast-breaking curl at the shoulder. The board is ridden with the tail in the curl. The white water breaking over the tail helps hold the board down when the rider moves forward to the nose. If the board races too far ahead of the break, the tail is freed from the downward push of wave and the nose will drop.

The type of board will also affect a hot-dogging perform-

The Quasimodo. One of the advanced positions of the riding forward style. Note how the breaking wave holds down the tail of the board and forms a tube over the surfer.

Toes on the nose. Surfer's rear foot is back and his weight is carried on it. Sometimes called the "Cheater Five" because the weight is not really forward, just appears to be.

ance. Boards that are long and heavy just won't perform in fast-breaking surf. If a board has too much *rocker* (pitch or bend) it will be too slow and will stall out easily, but it will hold up well when the surfer moves forward. A board with little or no rocker is quite fast but it will dig in and pearl with the slightest forward shift of balance. The beginner should pick a board with quite a large degree of rocker if he intends to do a lot of hot-dogging. Later, if the time comes to trade in the board for a new one, the more expert surfer may pick a board with a flatter bottom.

When a surfer decides he's going for the nose he moves forward as rapidly as possible. This is where the walk comes into play. The board must be kept in trim with the tail locked into the white water of the curl. The movement to the nose is done quickly and the position assumed immediately. To place five toes over the inside and forward rail, position the inside foot about eighteen inches from the nose and extend the outside foot right up to the point. Keep the weight on the rear foot to balance the board. As you reach this position, crouch as low as possible and gradually shift the weight forward. The stance can be held for fifteen or twenty seconds on a good wave—and then the wipe-out comes. To cut out of a nose ride, reach for the outside rail, take a good grip and then roll into the face of the wave. If the surf is not too large this pullout can bring the board and rider through the face of the wave and onto its back.

Another variation of the forward style is the parallel foot position. In this position both feet are forward and next to each other. The knees are bent and the surfer is almost in a squat. The feet are planted a foot or more from the nose and the inside foot is curled around the rail. Because the feet are almost parallel the legs look slightly bowlegged in the stance. Surprisingly this position works well and the rider is quite stable. From this position you can bring a foot back and shift your weight to the rear and bring the board into trim. Returning to trim and coming back to the more conventional

Feet forward and parallel—another nose riding position.

His fate is sealed. The board is pearling and the wave is closing out over him. These are the two main causes of hot-dogging wipe-outs.

Dick Gustafson

position is difficult. Most nose rides end with a combination pullout-wipe-out because they are usually held to the last possible moment.

The end of the nose ride usually occurs when a collapsing wave closes out over the rider. Sometimes it is possible to save the board from being washed away and pull out at the same time. At the end of the ride, fall or slide forward and off the inside of the board. Wrap the outside arm around the nose. As you fall into the face of the wave pull the nose of the board with you. The white water then pushes the tail around and you draw the board through the wave after you. This pullout only works in small to medium waves. In large surf the force of the wave won't permit you to punch through.

Hot-dogging has also found a place in competitive surfing. On small to medium waves expert hot-doggers show their styles to advantage at surfing meets. Competitors must make the somewhat unbalanced and quite difficult moves seem effortless. Nose riders who have learned to recover from the forward position can do several tricks on the same wave. For example, a simple feet forward and parallel crouch can be turned into a head dip or a quasimodo. After a head dip the surfer can stand, trim the board allowing it to stabilize and then walk the nose and finish the ride with *ten toes over*.

The speed at which the board is traveling will affect its stability and the ability of the rider to perform. If the board is mushing around in a slow lazy wave it won't be steady enough to support a forward riding position. If the wave is extremely critical and at the point of breaking across the front, there won't be time to move to the nose. The medium to small wave with a well-formed but fast-breaking shoulder is the hot-dogger's best choice.

Chapter 8

THE BIG SURF

ADVANCED surfing or *big-wave* riding means different things to different surfers. To the men who ride the Hawaiian winter surf it means waves over twenty feet high crashing in at places like Sunset Beach and Waimea Bay. In California big surf means a ten-foot day at Malibu or twelve feet at Wind and Sea, and on the East Coast seven feet at Virginia Beach is huge. The main difference between big surf and small surf is speed and size, but there are other differences. Big surf is usually more consistent, holds its form better, and places a much greater demand on the surfer.

In big surf the dangers are greater because of increased speed and more violent wipe-outs. A collision in a giant comber can involve a terrific impact between boards and surfers. Fortunately big waves are not so crowded and the riders are experienced. Riding the big surf calls for strong swimming ability. The bigger the surf the farther from the beach it breaks and the more currents created. Most of the famous big-wave surfers were competitive swimmers and beach lifeguards at one time. Peter Cole was one of the fastest swimmers in the United States twelve years ago. Cole worked many seasons as a beach lifeguard and still is one of the best all-around watermen. Big-wave riders Ricky Grigg, Buzzy Trent, Tom Zahn, Preston Peterson, and Dave

Rochlen, Sr., are all great swimmers and former beach life-guards. The demands placed on surfers by strong currents, towering waves, and long swims after a wipe-out are exhausting. Before attempting big surf, know that you are competent in the water and an expert swimmer.

Big Surf Technique

The change from riding small, shorebreak surf to large surf is like stepping from a skate board to a 500 cc motorcycle. When you have all that speed and power to contend with it's better to avoid mistakes. Your style on big waves must change because everything is moving faster and balance is harder to maintain. The big-wave surfer keeps his body slightly crouched on the board to lower the center of gravity and increase stability. This low position helps him handle sudden changes of board balance. As the board moves faster across the face of a large wave it pounds more. On a choppy windblown wave it is difficult to keep complete control of the board; and control is critical. A low stance also cuts down wind resistance. The legs help in a fast pounding ride by acting as shock absorbers. Look at photographs of good surfers riding big waves and you'll notice a great variety of stances, but these pictures all show the surfers standing with feet spread and knees bent and flexing to absorb shock. The loose flexible position also makes it easier to change board trim through body movement.

Since big surf is usually more consistent in form than smaller surf the rider has more time to think before acting. On shorebreak and smaller surf that's collapsing in front of the rider the decision must be reached instantly to pull out or try to make it. On larger waves the wall will hold longer, giving the surfer time to decide if it's best to pull out or try to make it across, or ride under the breaking crest of the wave.

Big surf is nothing new to shore dwellers and fishermen, and surfing a wave as a means of getting to shore is a com-

Gregg Noll streaks across a Waimea, Hawaii, giant, unaware of the
loose board behind him which could strike a deadly blow if it hit him.

monplace necessity for many coastal fishermen. The Cape
Cod dory is but one example of a boat built to work in and
out through the surf. Along the coast of Peru, running heavy
boats in and out through the surf is often the only way
freighters can be loaded and unloaded. Perhaps the most
interesting instance of big-wave surfing with an unusual
vehicle was experienced and described by Willard Bascom
in his book *Waves and Beaches*:

> Surfboarding on a Dukw [a six-wheeled army amphibious
> truck 32 feet long, pronounced Duck] is great sport. I well
> remember bucking out through the surf just south of the

Columbia River entrance, finally getting beyond the outermost breakers and then sitting there for nearly an hour getting up nerve enough to run the breakers. As a trough passed, we could look down a dark watery valley that disappeared into the fog in each direction; then we would be lifted up on the next crest. From this temporary vantage point we could see a dozen more huge crests approaching, and looking landward see the back side of lines of frightening breakers. They were all about the same—nearly twenty feet high. Finally we would pick what we thought were slightly lower waves and make a run for it. Usually our judgment of height was wishful thinking, but for excitement it beats a roller coaster any day: full speed ahead at six knots until you are overtaken by a wall of water as high as a house and moving three times your speed. The trick is to time the run so that the biggest wave breaks just barely ahead of you; then you can ride in atop the breaking crest, crossing the bar just in time to get beyond reach of the next wave. (It's a good idea, but it's hard to put into practice.)

As the wave overtakes the craft, there is a sickening moment when the stern begins to lift rapidly and the driver fights to remain square with the waves (encountering a wave sideways would mean disaster). Then as speed picks up, the craft tilts forward at thirty degrees or so and buries its bow until there is green water across the windshield. The entire craft seems about to flip end-over-end and you think, "Why did I ever get myself in a place like this? What a fool to go to sea in a truck!"

But then the wave begins to pass under, and the buoyancy of the forward end lifts the bow until it is a level platform projecting out ten to fifteen feet above the slick green water surface of the trough below. The forward wheels and axle hang down so that the rushing water of the breaker crests beats against them from behind and carries this awkward-looking truck-boat forward like a surfboard. Now you are flying, perched on a wave making fifteen knots, water boiling on all sides—an exhilarating ride.

Starting Out

Earlier we followed the progress of an imaginary surfer from his beginning wipe-outs. Let's find our friend Barney and see how he's doing. Barney has had about three good seasons of surfing experience and he's developed into an expert at his hometown beach. Barney has the local surf *wired*—he knows where to slide for the best ride, where and when to pick up good waves, and has even mastered most of the riding forward tricks. Barney has been itching to try big surf. He feels he's ready and recently he traded in his board for a *semi-gun* and wants to try it. Today he has found a new beach where the surf is humping up big and fast. Barney and a couple of friends arrive at dawn and look out to sea.

To their delight the surf is breaking almost a half mile out and the crests are holding beautifully. It looks so big their breakfast churns in their stomachs. Barney and his gung-ho friends unrack their boards and head for the beach. His buddies want to go out right away, but Barney has more respect for the surf. He's going to wait and watch. Twelve- to fifteen-foot surf is something new for Barney and he's playing it cautious. Shortly, a few of the local *big guns* arrive and paddle out. This is what Barney has been waiting for, a chance to watch the local experts perform and learn from them before committing a new board and a human body to the crunching effects of collapsing surf on an unknown rocky bottom.

The local experts wait for a lull between sets of waves. When the quiet period comes, they pick a channel and paddle out rapidly, thus avoiding a wipe-out and saving their energy for the coming rides. Once outside, the local surfers paddle beyond where the surf is breaking, an indication that they expect even larger waves and are staying farther out anticipating them. Barney observes that the local surfers know what they're doing because a big set is starting to build and they are in the perfect position for a good takeoff. The set comes. It's huge but not overly critical, nor overly steep. The surfers must make a hard aggressive effort to begin the glide. Nobody is taking off from the top. Barney guesses correctly that winds are making the top portion of the wave too bumpy for good control. The riders are holding their takeoff slide until they get about halfway down the slope of the wave and then they turn quickly.

One of the riders attempts making it through a tunnel, but the wave collapses and the unknown surfer is completely buried. Barney watches him carefully and counts to see how long he's driven under. One, two, three . . . nine, ten, eleven . . . and he's up. Barney knows now that a wipe-out won't bury him all morning, perhaps fifteen seconds at the most. This is long enough to be under if the wind is knocked out of you, but not long enough to be disastrous.

Overhead surf. Rider on left cuts away from break; surfer on right stalls.

Dick Gustafson

The wiped-out surfer makes it to the beach and Barney walks over to ask him about the depth of the water and the type of bottom. He learns that the water is deep enough to be safe during a wipe-out, though the bottom is rocky. The local surfer reminds him that it's now high tide, but by afternoon and low tide he'd better be careful of the rocks because it's shallow enough to hit bottom in a bad wipe-out.

Catching the Big Ones

Getting into the right position requires paddling out through heavy surf, getting close to where the wave peaks up, and moving to where a good shoulder forms. The takeoff on a large wave usually requires a hard driving paddle for sufficient momentum to begin to slide. If the wave is quite steep, a quick sprint paddle will start the slide. The conditions on each wave will determine where the slide should stop and the turn begin. When an offshore wind is blowing the crown off the wave, the turn is best held until the surfer has slid halfway or more down the wave face. This is when the bottom turn comes in handy. In the Hawaiian Islands where the offshore winds are intense, surfers have been blown off the tops of waves. Offshore winds also cause very choppy water along the crests, making control difficult. By dropping down the wave, more speed is obtained. This speed is needed to outrace the break. Some of the great surfers gain such speed that they are almost flying and just the last foot or so of their board is in the wave.

An aggressive driving takeoff followed by a determined turn help set the mood for challenging the wave and not letting its size and speed *psych out* the man trying to master it.

After the turn is made you must decide how long the wave will hold and what you're going to do with it. With a fast big wave board you can race ahead of the break, stall, turn back, and then shoot ahead again. Speed is critical and without it wipe-outs occur more often. The speeds reached on a wave depend on the skill of the surfer. By trimming the

A wipe-out in big surf. Surfer on left turns turtle; paddler in foreground faces an unpredictable loose board; diving surfer tries to escape crush of collapsing wave.

board correctly an expert big-wave rider picks up greater speed than a less experienced surfer who drags part of the board. The shape and length of the board, as well as its weight, contribute to attaining speed in big surf.

One of the reasons speed is so important in big surf is that most riders take off close to where the wave breaks. They need the long heavy boards to make the drop and pick up enough speed to race away. Surfing big waves with a hot-dog-type board often means the rider must place himself farther from the break where he'll have a better chance of outrunning the white water. If the surf is crowded, the people on the slower hot dog boards will usually be taking off in front of the big-board riders—and placing themselves in a likely position for a collision. A smashup in big surf is espe-

Sammy Lee heads for a vicious wipe-out as wave proves too steep to ride. Nose of board has pearled.

Ron Church

cially dangerous because the flying and diving boards are even wilder than usual. It's just not safe for a person on the inside, or farthest from the break, to take off in front of those already riding. He won't gain enough speed to stay in front of the other riders and will usually force them to pull out or collide.

Speed is really not so great in big surf, but the illusion of speed is tremendous, especially when the wind blows and the spray stings the eyes. A surfer named Bob Sheperd placed a marine speedometer on his board and measured speeds of around twenty miles an hour on six- to eight-foot waves at Sunset Beach. Speeds of thirty miles an hour are probably reached on larger waves. Hawaiian waves roll in faster than California or East Coast surf, where the continental shelf creates friction that slows the swells down.

Our friend Barney is about ready to ride his first big wave. It's early morning, conditions are perfect, and there are only a few surfers competing for waves. Barney has paddled out around the break, wisely taking the long route instead of trying to bust through and chancing a wipe-out before the first ride. His good sense also makes things easier for the surfers coming in. Once outside Barney double checks the best spot for the takeoff. He has noticed where the shoulder holds well and the drop won't be overly critical. Another surfer paddles next to Barney and spins about ready to catch the wave. The swell comes and to Barney's surprise the local surfer motions for him to take it. (Remember, this is fictitious.) Barney looks over his shoulder, sees the biggest swell he's ever thought of riding, and begins his paddle. He digs in hard and as his board picks up speed the wave comes. He feels like he's lifted a dozen feet and then the sudden drop down the face of the wave begins. Barney remembers not to stand too soon. He slides about halfway down, comes to his feet quickly but carefully, and makes a hard turn away from the break. He shifts his weight forward, trims the board carefully, and then his speed increases tremendously.

The Sequence of a Big Wave Ride

1.   Surfer takes off and comes to his feet. Weight is forward and he drops down face of wave before coming to his feet. Wave is so steep that surfer took off at an angle instead of down the face.

Ron Church

2.   On his feet and racing away from the cresting comber. The surfer
is still dropping and gaining speed to escape the break.

The ride is very fast and Barney lowers his body and
moves slightly toward the nose and goes into a slight crouch.
He quickly looks back and checks the break. He's surprised
to find he's out in front of it. He shifts his weight back, stalling and slowing the board. The break begins to catch up with
Barney and he moves forward and trims again, picking up

3. Wave continues to break, curl and form a tunnel. Rider has leveled off and trimmed the board for the utmost speed.

4. Wave has collapsed, but rider is beyond broken portion and racing for the safety of the shoulder.

Ron Church

speed. Now he's closer to shore and the wave is getting steeper and steeper. It's beginning to collapse around him and Barney pulls out. He uses his forward speed to carry him over the top of the wave and out of the break.

Over the wave Barney looks quickly out to sea. There's another wave coming and he has to escape it. He paddles with all the strength he's got and as the wave comes, he climbs, climbs, climbs, and makes it before it breaks. He's safe for awhile, but tired and shaking. Barney will paddle out a little farther and rest. Then he'll try again and again because he's hooked and he's conquered a big wave and something inside of him says it's been a day to remember for the rest of his life.

Chapter 9

COMPETITIVE SURFING

SURFING contests are as old as the sport itself, but mass participation in organized competition is an outgrowth of modern surfing. The Hawaiian surfers of Captain Cook's day were fiercely competitive. For the Hawaiian, surfing was a form of gambling. Contests were frequent and very large bets were placed; a man's entire possessions might depend on the way he rode a wave. The contests were also a means by which Hawaiian men demonstrated their prowess to the women. On some beaches the custom seems to apply to this day.

Competitive surfing events have multiplied in recent years. The West Coast leads in the number of meets, followed by Hawaii and Australia. The East Coast has summer and fall competition at Gilgo Beach (Long Island), Virginia Beach, Daytona Beach, and elsewhere. There are contests in France, South Africa, Peru, and, of course, the big one at Makaha, Hawaii. No single organization has yet brought order to these regional meets. There are several "International Surfing Championships," a "World Championship," and at least two West Coast Championships. The rules vary from beach to beach. The United States Surfing Association is attempting to develop standards for general adoption, but their constructive efforts have not yet impressed the surfing world, with the exception of the West Coast, which has adopted USSA rules.

A competitive surfer riding the white water. Note the wide spread of his feet as he tries to maintain control as the wave closes around him.

Allan Walker

The San Onofre Surfing Club of California has held meets since the mid 1930's. The first East Coast Surfing Championship was held at Daytona Beach, Labor Day, 1939. The 1963 East Coast Championship was held at Gilgo Beach. The latter drew contestants from Virginia, Delaware, Maryland, New Jersey, Connecticut, Rhode Island, and New York. The city of Babylon sponsored the contest. South America's Peru hosts a yearly Grand Championship in which there are three main surfing events, plus a paddling and swimming contest.

The growing popularity of these contests has brought about a jet set of surfers. Jet charter flights take teams and individuals from country to country to participate in meets, and many surfers follow the meets up and down the East and West coasts. As more funds become available to sponsor meets and surfers, the sport will take on some of the aspects of big-time golf. A distinction between professional and amateur surfers appears to be in the offing—and surfing is predicted to become an Olympic event in fifteen to twenty years.

There are also unofficial contests held without judges. These meets take place between individuals at the big wave beaches and determine over the season who is the best big-wave rider, the top hot-dogger, the most stylish surfer and perhaps the most aggressive surfer. The judges are the surfers themselves and the awards are not trophies, but reputation. The winners usually get movie jobs, or contracts to advertise surfboards, surf clothes, and other products.

Many of these same surfers also perform in official competition. The rider who is tops in the big surf may enter a contest when the surf is small and not even place. A surfer who is unknown, but who performs well on small waves, may win. Since there is still no universal definition of good or bad surfing style, a surfer who rides with a *pure* style may or may not be a better surfer than he who uses an extremely maneuverable up-and-down style. The surfers who usually win contests are the ones who can change their styles to fit the surf and the rules of a given contest.

Though some meets are specialized—limited to such events as tandem surfing, body surfing, or girls' surfing—most of the larger surfing contests include the following events:

Senior Men's Event (over thirty-five years)
Men's Event (sixteen years and up)
Senior Women's Event (sixteen and up)
Tandem Event (men with women partners)
Novice Tandem Event (for tandem teams who haven't
    placed in competition)
Boys' Event (fifteen years and under)

Extreme lean on the bottom turn. Left foot is on the edge of the inside rail and surfer's weight is shifting back during turn.

Allan Walker

Sliding right, a competitor crouches in his best form trying to pick up points from the judges. Note the good balance and the right rail of the board throwing a wake.

Team Paddling Event (teams sponsored by lifeguard services, athletic clubs or surfboard makers)

Dory Races (teams from lifeguard services or rowing clubs)

Singles Paddling (open to anyone)

Surfers are required to ride a certain number of waves in a specified time period. There may be five or six surfers in one heat; each must ride at least four waves and not more than six; the heat may last fifteen minutes or more. During the heats the judges must score each rider on each wave. Usually a ten-point score is used. A judge gives a rider any number of points between one and ten, one being the lowest. The judges must also consider the difficulty of the wave, the distance the wave is ridden, the skill and style of the rider, and his sportsmanship.

In California competition the United States Surfing Association supplies judges. They are respected members of the surfing world, and they are paid. There are usually five judges and three official scorekeepers at each meet. The USSA has developed an interesting "pre-packaged" surfing contest. Local communities contact the USSA; the USSA then comes to the community, supplies the officials, and runs the contest. USSA rules and regulations are followed.

The following list indicates the extent of international surfing competition today.

HAWAII

Makaha International Surfing Championships. Held for the last eleven or twelve years (exact date of inception unknown). The most representative "international" surfing meet yet. All types of events, and the surf is usually big at Makaha. The event was once called off for an hour because the surf was so good the judges couldn't resist taking off to ride a few themselves. Another time one of the judges left his stand and raced down the beach to rescue a drowning person whom nobody had noticed during the excitement of the contest.

AUSTRALIA

The Australia World Surfing Championship. Held in May at Sydney, Australia. Very international; surfers come from the United States, Great Britain, France, South Africa, Peru, and New Zealand. The last contest drew seventy thousand spectators, plus TV and radio coverage. One of the biggest surfing events yet.

PERU

Grand Championship of Peru. The first events take place in front of the Club Waikiki of Lima: Shorebreak hot-dogging and tandem. Then the contest moves to

Surf City—crowds at the U. S. Surfing Championships, Huntington Beach, California.

Kon-tiki Beach a half-hour drive from the club. Here the big surf is ridden. Draws surfers from the United States, Australia, and Hawaii.

UNITED STATES

California

1. Laguna Beach Surfing Tournament. An annual affair for the past eleven years. A top California contest, held in midsummer at the end of Brooks Street, Laguna Beach.
2. Oceanside Beach Annual U.S. Invitational Surfing Championships. Draws top surfers.
3. San Onofre Surfing Contest. Has been held since the mid-1930's. Here the youngest and oldest members of the surfing community compete in a very relaxed informal meet.
4. Huntington Beach United States Surfing Championships. Formerly called West Coast Championships, this is the biggest surfing contest in the United States. Draws the best surfers and the biggest crowds.

Eastern United States

There are several competitive events each summer and fall. Virginia Beach, Virginia, has a Surf Carnival each August. Gilgo Beach, Long Island, New York, and Daytona Beach each have yearly competition, as does Jacksonville, Florida. As yet no set pattern of surfing contests has developed on the East Coast, though both the numbers of meets and the surfers participating are growing each year.

The largest and best-organized surfing competition in the United States is the annual Huntington Beach contest. By 1964 this event had grown so large it was retitled "The United States Surfing Championships" because of the quality of the surfers and the size of the competition. The 1964

Three competitors caught inside fight to paddle over breaking wave. Surfer on the top was caught and went over backwards; other men made it through. Middle surfer is just beginning to turn turtle.

Allan Walker

124 THE COMPLETE BOOK OF SURFING

contest was held the weekend of September 26–27. A few days before the meet giant swells began rolling in from the south creating near-perfect surfing conditions. The surf held for the two-day meet and waves of eight and ten feet broke consistently. One TV cameraman was supported over the water in a metal cage that swung from the long boom of a crane parked on the Huntington Beach Pier.

The U. S. Surfing Championships started at dawn on Saturday and the last event was held late Sunday afternoon. Over four hundred surfers competed and several thousand spectators lined the beach and leaned over the rails of the pier. The competition drew men and women of all ages. The boys' division was won by Rodney Sumpter, a surprise entry from Australia. The overall winner was California surfer Mike Doyle, on a borrowed board. His own board smashed into the pier and snapped in half. The surf was that violent.

Again and again on both days the swells rolled in. The surfers had such an excellent choice of waves that each was able to give his maximum performance. The rides were so dramatic that spectators broke into cheers repeatedly.

An interesting sidelight of the Huntington Beach Championships was the requirement that competitors wear safety helmets. The crash hats served two purposes: they protected the surfers from possible head injuries and helped the judges identify contestants by the colors of the helmets' cloth coverings. The danger of a head injury due to collision with boards, rocks, or the bottom is always present, especially when the surf is crowded. In a recent United States Surfing Association Newsletter analysis of surfing fatalities (including body surfing), it was revealed that head injuries led to five drownings. These might have been prevented had the surfers worn crash helmets.

The helmets used at Huntington Beach were made of a fiberglass shell and polystyrene liner. This combination of fiberglass and foam offers remarkable impact protection. The helmet weighs only sixteen ounces and is designed to restrict the wearer's movements as little as possible. The helmet can also be used while motorcycling. In fact, it would be an asset for all types of boat racing and rough water aquatics. In case of accident the bright-colored hat would make the injured person easier to locate.

For further information regarding protective headgear for surfing or other aquatic sports write to: Surf-Helmet, Box 1313, Walteria, California.

Chapter 10

BODY SURFING

BODY surfing is the purest form of riding waves. Literally nothing stands between the surfer and the sea. Someone once described body surfing as "the closest thing to the great trauma of being born."

Body surfing can be done at almost any ocean beach where surf builds with sufficient strength and height. Waves of three feet and up breaking at least ten yards or more from the shore are required. You can catch a smaller wave, but it's not as much fun as riding a larger one. The only type of wave that can't be ridden is a crashing beach pounder that curls and dumps in shallow water, or a wave breaking in deep water without a steep face to slide on. Shorebreak dumpers are usually found at beaches where there is a rapid drop-off to deep water. If you wade out at these kinds of beaches you're over your head in a few steps. This is a warning that when large swells roll in they'll break close to shore quite violently. Shorebreak can be very dangerous. The best body surfing beaches are characterized by a gradually sloping bottom where the swimmer can walk out a long way from shore.

The principles behind catching a wave with the body are just about the same as for board riding. Let's examine what actually happens when a swimmer starts down a wave and his body begins planing and shooting for the beach. First, the body surfer is using the energy of the surf to move him. Second, he is being supported by the buoyancy of his body as it moves rapidly forward. With sufficient forward speed the body will rise and the chest and stomach and thighs will plane above the water. The larger the wave and the more forward velocity, the greater is the planing sensation.

The process of catching the wave is simple. The swimmer places himself in a spot just shoreward of where the wave will begin to break. Being in the right place at the right time is critical. If you're too far inshore of the cresting wave and it breaks, the forward slope will be destroyed, making the wave almost impossible to catch. If you try to pick up the wave too soon the face of the wave will not be steep enough to let the body start sliding. The body surfer has to pick up his wave at its steepest unbroken point in order to slide. Once the slide begins, the breaking wave gives the push to start the ride to the beach.

One of the major differences between board and body surfing is that the body surfer usually rides in the white water and the board surfer tries to avoid it. On a very steep, well-formed wave the body surfer can sometimes ride the shoulder of the wave just in front of the breaking portion. The beginner should stick to riding straight off until he develops more skill. Highly skilled body surfers can cut right or left, turn over in the wave, and ride it on their backs or their sides, and on a big wave even bring the arms out of the water and spread them like wings.

During the ride the body surfer has to keep track of what the wave is doing. Most waves dissipate gradually as they advance toward the beach. On waves with a potential to collapse violently the rider should pull out before getting dumped in the sand. The signal to pull out is a sudden dropping feeling combined with a sense of increased forward speed. In about half a second after the dropping sensation, your little world of wind, wave, and spray will end in a

Cecil Charles

Body Surfing. Both riders out in front and planing on their chests and stomachs.

Surfer drops her left shoulder and tries to slide into the unbroken portion of the wave.

shattering crash of collapsing wave. If the wipe-out is average the surfer will only have a bit of wind knocked out of him and maybe a little sand jammed in the eyes, ears, and nose. A bad wipe-out can break a collarbone, displace a shoulder, or bruise a person badly if he is dumped on the sand. People dumped in heavy shorebreak have even suffered broken backs and necks. All these hazards can be avoided by a quick pullout that should begin before, or just as, the wave collapses. A body surf pullout is as simple as dropping a shoulder or rising up to decrease speed and letting the wave pass by. Many body surfers pull out of a wave by doing a forward roll when they come close to the beach. The forward roll into the *cannonball* position is good protection against being dumped; the blow is taken on the shoulder and the head is protected. When forward rolling, the chin should be tucked to the chest and the knees drawn up. By all means try to avoid landing on the head. The shock can be disastrous to the neck and back.

Let's follow an experienced body surfer on a trip to the beach and see how she goes about it. Ann, our teacher for today, arrives at Beach X with fins to help her get started in case the surf is breaking in deep water. She wears a bathing cap. Ann has surfed at Beach X many times and knows the bottom is free from rocks, old pipes or any other hazards that the body surfer might run into. She also knows this beach forms the best waves at medium tide. Today medium tide is about noon, tomorrow it will be an hour or so later. Each day the tide changes, the time and degree varying widely, depending on location.

Shallow water is the best place to begin. When the body surfer is standing where his feet touch bottom he can use the leg muscles to push himself to a forward-moving prone position. If the depth of the water is chin level or above, it's too deep and the legs can't get much leverage to push out. Chest-deep water is about the maximum depth for a good standing start. The push, the strong fast stroke, and the kick are necessary to achieve the initial speed to start the slide.

Ann has picked a spot in chest-deep water. Here the surf is about three feet high and is breaking consistently. The break is smooth and the shoreward rush of wave is fast enough to carry a person toward the beach. Ann keeps an eye "outside" for a good wave. She may move seaward or shoreward jockeying for a better position. Body surfers don't stand rock-still waiting for the perfect wave. They swim, twist, dive, and constantly fight for the right spot to catch a wave. Unless the surf is coming in consistently there is usually time to judge the wave and move to the best position to catch it. As in board surfing, there's always a bigger wave coming and the alert surfer keeps an eye to the horizon watching for it.

Ann has spotted a wave. It's building up a little larger to her right and will break out farther than where she stands. Ann moves out to meet it, either by swimming or a combination of swimming and walking her way through the water. She has to use judgment and decide what will be the best spot to meet the wave before it starts breaking. Ann arrives a second before she must start the ride. There is just time to turn shoreward, look over her shoulder for a last check of the wave, and then kick off. Either one or both legs are used to kick off, depending on the position of the body. When she pushes off the bottom, several things happen at once. She takes a hard, deep pulling stroke with one arm. This stroke, combined with the push-off, brings her body off the bottom and nearly parallel to the surface and starts it moving forward. This is not a gentle, refined movement, but almost a violent struggle to match the speed and power of the wave. The start begins just as the wave is about to break and is at its steepest position. The steep face of the wave raises the feet and begins to tilt the body forward and downward. On the next stroke Ann drops her head, hunches her shoulders forward so her chest is slightly concave, and tips the upper torso downward. The downward tilt of the body is very important because it starts the slide as the wave supplies the water to slide on. If the head and shoulders are dropped too low the body will pearl just like a surfboard. If the head and shoulders are held too high the body will stall out of the wave, again just like a surfboard that is overbalanced at the tail. After the slide starts—and there's no mistaking this feeling—the head is raised and the body begins planing. On a fast powerful wave the planing action will support the upper body so the shoulders and chest will rise out of the water. If the wave slows down and the surfer feels he is falling out of it, he can drop his head and shoulders, increase his downward angle, and pick up speed. This is like dropping the nose of the surfboard to trim it and go faster.

On another day the surf might be bigger and breaking farther out from shore. Let's return Ann to the beach and see how her body surfing style changes as the condition of the surf changes. On this particular day the surf is perfect at Beach X, good swells are coming in and the surf is humping up and breaking about thirty yards from the beach. To casual visitors the surf appears five or six feet high, but Ann knows waves usually look bigger than they really are. Her guess is about four feet and she's correct. Ann notices that the waves are breaking from the top and rolling shoreward with a consistency that means the rides will be smooth. No bone-crushing shorebreak today. Ann also knows that the surf is breaking in water over her head. To the body surfer a deep-water start means two things. First, there is no bottom to get a push-off from. Second, something must help start the body moving down the face of the wave in order for the slide to start. In deep, over-the-head water the swim fins give the push, the initial high-speed start, that kicking off from the bottom does in shallow water.

Some body surfers start by swimming in the backstroke position. They like to be on their backs in order to see the wave. When the swell comes they are already moving and can flip over to a crawl position and take off.

Swim fins also help you stay in the wave if it starts to slack off. Sometimes on a big wave there is a lull in its action before the final rush to the beach. The swim fins give the added speed so you can continue riding until the force of the wave carries you along again. Also fins help you to turn when you reach the point that sliding right or left is possible.

Ann has watched the surf a few minutes and decided where it's breaking best. She's on her way out now. Her swim fin heel straps are looped over her wrist to keep them from being torn from her hand as she goes through the surf. Walking with fins in shallow water is quite difficult. It's easier to put them on in deeper water. Ann has also (girls please note) knotted the straps of her bathing suit top before hitting the surf. She knows the power of waves and wants to prevent any embarrassment. (After eight seasons as a beach lifeguard, the author has seen this "embarrassment" enough times to be able to keep a straight face when taking a young lady a towel.)

On the way out Ann walks until she reaches chest-deep water. Body surfers and beach lifeguards know it's faster and easier to wade out to chest-deep water than to swim. In big surf this also enables the swimmer to watch the advancing waves. Ann's in a hurry now—she has seen a big set coming and wants to get outside before the inrushing waves swamp her. She moves quickly, timing her entrance between waves so she will reach water deep enough to dive under if a breaker should collapse on her. One wave of the incoming set holds up longer than the rest and breaks in front of Ann. Rushing toward her in a wall of white water with sufficient power to knock her down and tumble her back. The water-wise girl moves to meet it. Just before the white water engulfs her she dives forward under the wave. Her dive is shallow, just deep enough to carry her along the bottom. She's trying to place as much water as possible between herself and the wave to cushion the shock. Ann rides the outbound countercurrent seaward until well past the broken

Body surfer races breaking shoulder of large Hawaiian wave.

wave. When she surfaces she takes a quick breath, checks for another crasher, and then starts swimming out.

Once beyond the break, Ann treads water slowly waiting for just the right wave. When body surfing big waves, the surfer normally waits for a particularly good wave—the swim back for a poor one is just too much wasted energy. Also in deep water it's harder to maneuver to a good position for a takeoff. Ann's wave comes and she sets herself for it. It looks great; just before it reaches her the crest seems to throw itself skyward. An instant before the white water begins Ann starts working her fins. She holds off stroking for a moment until she is sure she is about to catch the wave. Then Ann takes one powerful stroke, putting all she can into the arm pull. Taking only one stroke is important in big surf; another will only create resistance instead of momentum.

In deep water there is little danger of a bad wipe-out, unless coral or rocks lie below the surface. Sometimes on a big wave the drop during the start seems rather steep, but that's only the illusion of height a big wave gives. It's an exciting soul-filling feeling to really hook into a big wave, take the drop and race toward the beach at fifteen or twenty miles an hour.

There is more to body surfing than style and technique. There are feelings that must be experienced to be understood. Planing in on a six-foot wave that broke fifty or sixty yards from shore can make you feel like an express train racing across the plains. Letting out a great yodel and grinning at your friends on the beach as you ride head and shoulders out of the white water can make you feel as if you're on top of the world. And if you're as lucky as some people have been you may look over your shoulder and see a seal grinning at you as it skims along in the same wave. Body surfing is a sport of spills and thrills and great roaring boisterous good fun. Try it.

Chapter 11

SURF MATS, BELLYBOARDS, AND DORIES

ONE of the fascinating aspects of surfing is that waves can be ridden with all sorts of floats, boats, and other aquatic devices. A wave can be caught with almost any floating object that will slide down the front of a breaker. The white water can also be used to push along inflated things such as cloth, air-filled mattress covers, inner tubes or other types of buoyant floats. However, surf mats and bellyboards are the primary surfing devices for riding big waves and performing tricks. The surf mat is a rubber-coated canvas float that is rectangular in shape. Surf mats are quite strong and when rigidly inflated they slide with almost the same speed as a surfboard.

Bellyboards are really little surfboards. Several types are now in use—some are simply flat pieces of wood with a rounded nose and others have one or two skegs. The modern commercially made bellyboard is like a full-size surfboard, except the dimensions have been scaled down. Both mats and bellyboards are propelled with swim fins on feet and arms paddling.

Waves can also be ridden using canoes, kayaks, dories, sailing catamarans, and with certain types of outboard motorboats. If the surf is breaking gently and spilling gradually forward, almost anything that floats, and can develop sufficient speed to start the slide, will catch a wave. The author has surfed a 28-foot powerboat, dories, and once rode a wave in an eight-man oceangoing lifeboat. Even an amphibious truck can be surfed. Surfing a boat, or even a specially designed surfing dory, takes skill that can only be learned from long exposure to waves and surfing. Most boats are not designed to surf and it's just not safe to try it unless wave conditions are perfect. Anyone bringing a boat in to the beach had better keep it just behind the breaking wave and not get tangled up in the white wave. A boat broaching in the surf line (turning sideways) will normally dump over and toss the passengers out or trap them inside the hull; if the surf is big the boat is usually destroyed. Surf mats and bellyboards are a different matter, however; they are both fun to surf and quite safe.

Riding the Surf Mat

Surf mats have long been a favorite surf-riding device on both coasts of the United States, in Hawaii, and in Australia. Many of today's top surfers had their first wave ride bouncing along atop a rubber-canvas surf mat. The mats normally come in two sizes, junior and adult. Some are moderately priced, but the best cost up to $18 or $20. The imported mats are inferior in quality. The best ones are made by the U.S. Rubber Company and the Hodgeman Company. A good surf mat lasts many years, if kept out of the sun after use and allowed to dry slowly.

Mat surfing on small mats is ideal for children provided they remain in the white water. Experienced swimmers can take the mats farther out to catch full-size waves and ride the shoulder at an angle—just like a surfboard. Lightweights and experienced children can also ride mats on their knees and some youngsters have even learned to stand while riding.

The simplest way to catch a wave with a surf mat is to stand in shallow water and as the broken wave approaches

Sliding a big one—at least it's big for this young man. The boy is water-wise and keeps his weight back so the front of the mat won't dig in and pearl.

A water-wise youngster tosses his surf mat over the wave so the inrush of water won't sweep it away from him.

jump on the mat. When jumping on, give a push with the legs so the mat shoots forward. At the same time kick energetically. The push of the inrushing wave will scoot mat and rider right up to the dry sand. As the mat surfer gains experience he can make deep-water starts for the larger unbroken waves. A deep-water start requires the mat to be moving just like a surfboard. To get the mat going, fins are a great help. Fins also aid the mat surfer in kicking out to where the surf is breaking. If the surf is big and the inrush of broken waves quite strong, it is difficult to work the mat through the white water position. Most mats have a rope bridle at one end which can be used to tow the mat seaward. The rope is also used to pull the nose of the mat up while sliding. This keeps the front end from digging in and pearling on the slide to shore. Some mat surfers toss the mat over the incoming wave, dive under the break, surface on the other side and recover the mat. Once the mat and rider are outside the breaking surf and ready to catch a wave, there are a few points to remember: 1) Mats don't paddle as fast as surfboards and the rider must place himself as close to the break as possible; 2) when the wave comes the mat is positioned so the takeoff will be straight off from the wave, and the turn, if made, is done after the wave is caught; 3) the weight is kept forward during the initial part of the ride to start the slide down the wave face, and 4) when the slide actually starts, the weight is shifted back and the nose of the mat is pulled up to prevent pearling.

Mat surfing is relatively safe. Bad wipe-outs in crashing shorebreak surf present the only real dangers. If the waves are curling and dumping right on the beach, surf somewhere else or wait till these conditions change. Another hazard of mat surfing, or any kind of surfing where children are concerned, is that strong offshore winds sometimes blow the mat and rider seaward. On some public beaches where offshore winds are common, any kind of floating object, such as inner tubes, is prohibited.

Mats can be repaired with a tire patch if they develop a leak. A mat can be stowed in the trunk of a car, inflated, and used whenever visiting the beach. It's best to roll up a mat after use instead of folding it; some wear will occur at the corners where the fold bends the fabric.

The Bellyboard

The bellyboard is really just a short surfboard. Years ago bellyboards were short wooden planks with rounded ends. Surfers made the start while standing on the bottom and always rode the bellyboard in the white water.

The modern bellyboard has grown a skeg, a covering of fiberglass and an inner core of foam. These are very fast, and on the right wave they can go faster than a surfboard. In Hawaii the bellyboards are called *paipos* and are ridden right along with surfboards, even in the big surf at Sunset Beach. Because the bellyboard is much lighter than a surfboard the ride is somewhat rougher on big waves, but equally thrilling. On medium-size, well-formed waves the little boards are ideal; in fact they're almost as much fun as riding a conventional surfboard. The terrific speed obtained on a bellyboard makes it somewhat harder to pull out of a breaking wave. So pullouts should be started a little sooner, before the wave closes over the surfer.

Since bellyboards are harder than surfboards, wipe-outs and collisions are potentially more hazardous. Bellyboards pearl more easily than mats because trim is more critical and they are less buoyant. The fat forward edge of a surf mat doesn't dig in as easily as the sharper and thinner nose of a bellyboard. In fact mats can take a very steep drop without pearling. In many cases surf mats will turn end over end before they pearl, but of course mats aren't as fast or as maneuverable. Bellyboards are also a little harder to move through the water and fins are needed to kick to where the surf is breaking, and to make a deep-water start. It's also important to position the bellyboard as close to the breaking portion of the wave as possible. The principle of the start is the same for bellyboards and surfboards, except that there is less margin for error in positioning with the bellyboard.

When the ride is almost over, remember to pull out before the wave breaks up on the beach. A wipe-out in the shore-break can tear the board away, and it may fly into the air and land on your head. Pulling out of a wave is simple: you roll into the face of the wave and let it pass by. Try to retain the board. If it gets away and bounces in to shore with the white water it may strike someone.

Dory Surfing

Dories have been standard surfboats for hundreds of years. The current Cape Cod dory, for instance, evolved from an eleventh-century Scandinavian design. The dory, sometimes called a *double ender,* can be identified by its raised and pointed bow and stern (the modern dory has a sharper bow point than stern point). The high sharp bow and the deep V sides that flatten on the bottom explain why dories are such good surfboats. Heading into surf, the high bow knifes through waves and then, on the way back to shore, it prevents pearling. If a wave breaks to the rear, the sharp stern splits its force so that the water cannot break over and flood the boat.

Rowing or surfing a dory is an art. Most dories have two-man crews, a bowman and a sternman. The stern oarsman is captain; he makes the decisions and gives the order to take a wave or not. On the way in through the surf, the sternman steers the dory and in his hands lies the safety of the boat and the oarsmen. He usually stands and rows when launching through the surf or coming back to the beach. This position gives him better vantage for watching and judging the surf. When a wave is caught, the bowman ships his oars and sets himself for the ride in. It's a thrilling sight to watch a good doryman come through the surf. If the sternman is experienced he'll stand with great composure and commit

Ron Church

Bellyboarding a good-size wave. The surfer has caught the shoulder and is riding at an extreme angle. Note his left fin is dragging, turning him left.

Dories in action: The start of a lifeguard dory race at Zuma Beach, California.

the boat to the surf at just the proper moment. With only one or two strokes, the sternman starts the dory in the slide— and the wild watery sleigh ride begins. The sternman guides the boat by dipping an oar left to turn left, right to turn right.

Many of the skills of board surfing apply also to dory surfing. Judging a wave is even more critical in dory surfing. A wave that is crashing cannot be ridden by a boat; waves must spill gradually from the top and roll forward breaking gently. Dorymen wait for exactly the right wave, even if it means long periods of time. Their boats are handmade and expensive and a misjudged wave can mean a smashed boat and injured oarsmen.

As a swell comes up behind the boat, both bowman and sternmen pull on their oars together. The dory is a quick starter because it's light. In a few strokes it matches the speed of the swell and begins to slide. Once a dory is committed to the surf there is no pulling out. The wave must now be ridden all the way to the beach. Good dorymen end their ride by spinning the boat, using the power of the wave to shove the hull around so that it points out to sea again for the next trip out.

If the dory broaches in the surf line and turns over, bail out and get clear of oars and falling boat. But when the dory is merely slammed sideways by the surf and doesn't feel as if it's about to turn over, then stay with the boat and hang on. Keep the body as low as possible. This maintains balance and keeps the boat from turning over.

Chapter 12

SKIM BOARDING, BOAT WAKE
SURFING AND SKATEBOARDING

ALONG the shores of Southern California, Hawaii and the southeast coast of the United States skim boarding is very much a part of the beach scene. Riding a skim board is simple to define, difficult to accomplish: you jump on a fast-moving circle of plywood and slide along on a few inches of water the spent waves have provided.

Skim boarding was probably developed in the Hawaiian Islands by young children trying to imitate their surfing fathers by riding a flat piece of driftwood. Some early beachcomber may have noticed the children riding the discs and upon his return to the mainland astonished local bathers by sliding down the berm as if riding on the balls of his feet. People who have lived around the beaches for years can't recall who started skim boarding or just when it began, but say it has always seemed to be part of beach recreation.

The skimboard is a round or oval plywood disc. To understand the principle of the skimboard, picture in your mind a boat's hull planing across the water. When the boat starts out, the stern sits deep in the water and drags until planing speed is reached. Then the boat rises on the hull and begins to speed. Once planing occurs, the boat only draws a few inches of water and overcomes much of the water's resistance. The skim board utilizes this planing action, and the

143

faster it is launched from the rider's arms the faster it will go and the less water it will displace. Rides of a hundred feet and more are possible if the rider gets a good start.

Select the right stretch of beach. A good *berm* (slope) for skim boarding must slope gently seaward, so gently that the water remaining after a wave has spent itself takes several seconds or longer to wash back. The beach should be free from rocks, pebbles or gravel. A pebble or small rock catching on the bottom of the skim board will slow or stop it while the rider keeps on going—usually to a hard wet fall on the sand. Before skim boarding, always check the area you intend to use. The best time for skim boarding is low tide, unless the beach has a very gentle slope.

The skim board is held in both hands and slightly in front and to one side of the body. The board, or disc, is kept parallel to the beach with a slight tilt upward. The rider begins to run and as he reaches a good speed he crouches closer to the sand. Just as a wave deposits a few inches of water on the sand the running rider throws the board gently ahead of himself so it lands flat. In the next few steps the rider runs with the board and then hops on. This is the critical point. The rider must match the speed of the skim board and he must land on it gently, so gently that the board does not sink but continues its glide. The weight of the rider should be placed slightly to the rear of the board so the nose will not dig in. The leading edge of the skim board is just out of the water and it throws a small wake, like a boat. As long as there is sufficient water for the board to glide on, and momentum, the ride will continue. Long rides are possible if the slope is gentle. The skim board will move ahead and gradually run down the slope until it runs into deeper water or dry sand.

Two techniques make learning to skim board easier. One, called the *crab position*, works well when teaching children. The board is carried at a run, tossed ahead and the child jumps on. Instead of standing, the child drops to his knees.

A skimboard finish.

Another way of skim boarding. The rider is flying along in the prone position at 10 to 12 miles an hour.

Dick Gustafson

This lowers the center of gravity, makes balance easier, and the child can get the feeling of the slide and glide. Another method: hold the child's hand and run with him. As the child jumps on the skim board, hold his hand and help him maintain his balance. Continue to run along holding the child's hand. If the board comes to an abrupt halt, you can keep the child from falling. Always warn a beginner to anticipate an abrupt stop as the board grabs into dry sand. The rider must leap off and continue ahead at a run. The feeling is like stepping off a moving streetcar or train; if the passenger doesn't step nimbly and match the speed of the train, he is likely to fall.

A novel variation of skim boarding is *skimming*. Skimming thumbs its nose at the plywood board and replaces it with the rider's own stomach. It's rather tricky: the body must be launched through the air, landed on the water, and sent gliding. Skimming takes guts, skill, and a certain disregard for bruised noses and the skin on your chest. The sport isn't recommended for girls over the age of twelve or for the weak of heart, or the sane.

Building a Skim Board

Making the disc is as simple as cutting a circle of plywood 30 to 40 inches across out of a larger sheet of wood. The size will depend on the weight of the rider. The plywood should be first-quality, waterproof marine grade, and free from blemishes. A lumberyard band saw can cut a perfect circle, and the 50 cents milling fee most lumberyards charge is worth it for a precise cut. The wood should be five ply and ⅝ inch thick. Thinner wood is too flexible and weak; thicker plywood is too heavy. The edges of the wood should be sanded round and free from splinters. Give the disc two or three smooth coats of high-grade marine varnish. Apply canning paraffin to the top, or riding surface, to insure good traction for the feet.

A final word—watch out for dogs. They seem to regard

the skim boarder in the same category as the postman or the paper boy on his bike.

Boat Wake Surfing

Surfing on the wake created by a powerboat has opened up a new world of water sport for inlanders. On almost any body of calm water deep and large enough to support a good-sized outboard, people can now surf. The idea of using a boat-created wave isn't new, but the surfboards to ride the wake are. Most boats create only small waves, but the fun is still there and valuable surfing skills can be developed. Since wake surfing is new, no one really knows what the limits are. It may be possible to hook on the wake of an ocean liner or ride behind a Great Lakes ore ship. One surfer successfully rode the wake of a 90-foot fishing boat. He managed to ride along at fifteen knots, and stated that the ride was fantastic.

Dr. Willard Bascom recounts wake surfing on the Hudson River before World War II. Using a canoe, he and other boys rode the wake behind a ferryboat. In 1956, Marge Calhoun, one of the great women surfers, began wake surfing. Pete Peterson, surfing's "Iron Man," used to hitchhike his way to Catalina Island behind a large steamer, using a small boat to ride the wake. Porpoise and dolphin have learned to ride below the bow wake of ships. These naturally buoyant animals with their remarkable intelligence have grasped the physics of surfing and appear to ride miles and miles with little or no effort. Freeboarding was another early sport done behind a boat, but the surfer held a rope and rode the surfboard like a water skier.

Wake surfing was given its initial impetus as a sport by Dick Pope of Cypress Gardens, Florida. One day while towing surfboards behind a boat, he saw the possibilities of wake surfing and gave it a try. The Johnson outboard motor people thought wake surfing would be a good device to promote motor sales and provided cameras and equipment to document the boat surfing technique. Soon the surfing magazines were running articles. Word spread—and wake surfing became big sport in a single summer. Such is the age of mass communications.

Today boards are being designed expressly for wake surfing. They're slightly smaller than conventional surfboards and of lighter construction. One company, Plastic-Mart of Santa Monica, California, is already producing a do-it-yourself wake board kit. Their design follows the conventional surfboard closely except that the stringer has been omitted; less longitudinal strength is needed.

A few Southern California lifeguards have even tried body surfing in a boat's wake. They don't recommend it, though—the body surfer has to ride too close to the propeller to stay in the wake.

Wake surfers can perform many of the stunts of conventional surfers. You can cross over the wake and back again. You can execute cutbacks, stalls and other turns. Since boat surf is small, there's little danger of wipe-outs or collisions. There are hazards, though, just as in water skiing. Crossing in front of other boats is to be avoided, the propeller is always a potential hazard and a spill in shallow water can injure the rider.

A fairly large boat is required to build sufficient wake for surfing. Most 17-footers with a 75-horsepower motor or a pair of smaller engines will throw a fine wake. If additional weight is placed in the stern, say about four or five friends, or sandbags, the back of the boat will settle deeper in the water and create a large wake. Speed isn't as important as size in wake surfing. Most boats will begin to throw a surfable wake at about ten to twelve miles an hour. Above fifteen or sixteen miles an hour the boat will begin to plane, the characteristics of the wake will change, and the surfer will lose the wave. A little experimentation is required to determine how each individual boat will behave. On the wake of a larger boat several people can ride together. Tandem surfing is also possible, and what a way to practice the stances—no bad wipe-out and no having to paddle back out and wait for a wave.

Riding the Wake

Getting started is easy as grabbing a towline, hanging on until the board begins to plane in the wave and then letting go. The start must be gradual, and the boat operator must be careful not to create too great a strain on the surfer's arms. Your weight should be back far enough so that the nose of the board won't dig in and pearl. If the water is choppy, it is harder to keep from taking water over the nose. A calm, glassy water surface is best.

You start either prone or on the knees. As the boat gathers speed, the board becomes more stable and you can stand. Coming to the feet is done just as on a regular wave. The quicker the stand is made, the less likely the board will tip and the rider fall. You can lean back slightly, letting the rope

"Midget" Farrelly, top Australian surfer, ready to catch a wake wave. He starts from his knees keeping the nose of the board up.

Dick Gustafson

Here the wake surfer has caught the wave and is coming to his feet. He still holds the rope in case he slips out of the wave. The rope is knotted to provide a better grip.

support some of your weight. This is a bit like starting on water skis, except that there is not as much resistance because the larger bottom surface of the board slides through the water with less friction.

After you are on your feet, experiment to find the best balance spot. The rope is held all this time. If the weight is too far back, the tail of the board will dig in and you will

Dick Gustafson

The remarkable woman surfer Marge Calhoun and "Midget" Farrelly share the same wake. Farrelly is in the wave and his rope is slack. His partner's rope is taut, indicating she is not yet in trim and sliding.

Both riding the wake and in trim now. Their balance is slightly forward to help trim in the small wake.

Dick Gustafson

This is free boarding. When wake surfing becomes a little slow, some surfers keep the rope and have the boat pull them at high speed.

find the rope pulling quite hard; if too far forward, the nose will dig in and pearl. Sometimes you will be too far behind the wake and will have to pull the board forward into the wave. You—or someone in the boat—can do this by taking up the slack in the rope. On the other hand, if you get too close to the boat, the stern watch can let out extra rope.

Once the boat is moving fast enough and the wake has built to its largest size, get ready to drop the rope and catch the wake wave. As in natural wave surfing, the start must be combined with a drop of the board's nose down the face of the wave. In wake surfing the downward angle is quite slight. All it takes to drop the nose is a slight leaning forward movement. If this fails to change the balance sufficiently, take a step or shuffle toward the nose.

When the slide begins—and this feeling can't be missed—

Hot-dogging on a boat wake wave. Here is the head dip.

the rope will go slack and the board will seem to speed up slightly. At first, hold the rope until you get the feel of wake surfing. If you slide back out of the wave, the rope will stop you from losing the boat and you won't have to start from a dead stop all over again.

Trimming the board is important in wake surfing. There is very little wave face to work on so you must be careful not to drop too far back in the wake. If you cut too far from the edge of the wake, you'll likely lose the riding crest. Once you are standing and riding free of the rope's pull, the boat operator can increase speed until the wave is destroyed as the boat planes. The operator can then slow and judge the best throttle setting for wake surfing. There should also be an observer in the stern to keep an eye on the surfer—a good safety precaution.

Trim in wake surfing is rather different from trim in an ocean wave. The board is more parallel to the water's surface in wake surfing, and there isn't as much up or down motion. Essentially, the board is kept flat. Turns and other maneuvers are not done with gross movement, but are kept down to small, more precise changes of balance. The transition from ocean surf to wake surf is easy for an experienced surfer, but it is a bit difficult for the beginner. Since paddling isn't stressed in wake surfing, the beginner has no opportunity to get the feel of the board and learn how to balance it. Some preliminary work in paddling will help the novice learn faster.

Skateboarding

The skateboard has become the "Link Trainer" or teaching machine for many young surfers, and a retraining device for accomplished surfers. Even skiers use the skateboard for preseason training. The skateboard is nothing more than a three-foot hardwood surfboard with a set of high-quality roller-skate wheels firmly attached to the bottom. Skateboards are not new; but using expensive rubber or hard plastic roller-bearing wheels is. Since the early days of roller-skating, kids have attached worn-out wheels to boards and scooted along city sidewalks. They worked well, but the modern skateboards are much better because of good wheels that can accommodate radical turns.

Skateboards have captured the imagination of thousands of pre-surfers and inlanders who want to experience the thrill of surfing. The wheeled miniature surfboard also provides a means of simulating the movements a skier makes on his long thin skis. The growth of skateboarding has paralleled the growth of surfing. It is a form of recreation that can be practiced on any level patch of concrete or asphalt.

In California the producers of the Makaha Skateboard, a three-man company, had to hire twenty extra employees to fill their Christmas orders. Hundreds of youngsters are forming skateboard teams, clubs, and local contests. The stunts performed on skateboards are limited only by the physical ability of the riders. Some riders are doing handstands, some are speed racing, and others are even high jumping from a moving skateboard, clearing the bar, and then landing on the board.

Is skill required? Just normal balance and legs that can run and jump. A skateboard moves quickly. It gains momentum because the rider gives it the initial start and keeps it going with a push from one leg.

To start the skateboard moving the rider takes a short quick run and jumps aboard. The board can also be started from a standstill by placing one foot on the board and pushing with the other foot. The skateboard also turns very rapidly as the rider shifts his weight from side to side. Like the surfboard the skateboard is turned by a change of balance brought about by a lean in the direction the rider wishes to turn.

Just as in surfing, there are two styles of skateboarding: the hot-dogging fast-turning style and the straight-off big-wave style. Hot-doggers perform their fast turns, spinners, nose rides, and other tricks on flat pavement. The big-wave style is practiced on hills, the steeper the better. San Francisco is the ideal spot for downhill skateboarding. Terrific speeds are obtained riding down steep hills, but this style can be dangerous. Abrupt stops send the rider flying, and a spill into the path of oncoming cars is a special danger.

As in surfing and skiing, the skateboarder should keep himself under control at all times. As any other fast-moving athlete, the skateboarder should look and plan ahead. The intersection of roads, the break in the pavement, the loose gravel and the too sharp turn are all potential hazard areas. Speed is not all that important. Don't forget style and grace and safety . . . and fun.

Chapter 13

SURFING AREAS

SURF breaks wherever the seas beat against the world's coastlines. In some areas the surf is perfect for riding waves, in others impossible, and in still others good surf forms but has yet to be discovered. When one considers the thousands and thousands of miles of coastline bordering the world's land masses there are unlimited possibilities of finding new surfing areas. As the number of surfers grows they will move farther and farther afield in the search for surf. One authority stated that the only two places where surfing may not be possible are the Arctic and the Antarctic. One of the major surf film producers recently went on a round-the-world surf-filming safari and found ideal wave conditions in Africa and Japan as well as on other remote coastlines. The western coast of France has opened up as one of the better surfing areas. The author found very favorable surf conditions on the coast of Portugal, and as far as is known nobody has yet surfed the waves of that little country.

Today there are certain recognized areas where the waves are more or less consistently good for surfing. The major areas are Hawaii, California, Australia, the eastern coast of the United States, New Zealand, South Africa, Peru, Mexico and the west coast of France.

If you happen to be in a coastal area where there are no surfers to provide information on the best and safest places to slide, do some detective work. A seaman's chart of the local coastline will show rocky points or reefs that might start surf breaking. Look for gradually descending bottoms, reef outcroppings close to shore, or projecting land that might start a point break. Then find an eyewitness. A local fisherman should be able to describe the surf accurately. He could tell if the surf is the crashing or spilling type or if a shoulder forms and the waves roll in. Lifeguards and Coast Guard personnel also know surf conditions intimately.

The big surf beach of Kon-tiki, Peru, was discovered by an airline pilot who recognized the area's potential while flying overhead. The late Bob Simmons used to scan U. S. Coast and Geodetic Survey aerial photos to discover new surfing areas.

Here are the best and most accessible surfing spots:

California

California surfing begins at Santa Cruz south of San Francisco and extends south into Mexico. Though people do surf in Oregon and Northern California, the water is extremely cold all year and surfing areas are few and far between. From Santa Cruz south, people surf the year around, but from November to June a wet suit top is essential. Below Los Angeles, the water is slightly warmer in the winter and the hardy surfer can take the cold most days when the sun is out. California and northern Mexico (Baja California) also respond to the direction of swell. In the summer the south swell makes certain beaches better for surfing than others which break well from a north swell. Rip currents and reefs are a problem. So are crowds. During the summer weekends the competition for a ride is fierce. But there are many beaches, and with a half day's driving, the crowds can be avoided. The farther one drives from the metropolitan center of giant Los Angeles, the less dense the crowds.

Santa Cruz. This extensive surfing area is south of San Francisco and on the north end of Monterey Bay. Santa

Cruz has two distinctive features: the surf is excellent and the water is very, very cold. Santa Cruz has been surfed since before World War II, but has really grown in popularity in recent years. The surf at Cowell's Beach is good for beginners due to the gradual break which is somewhat similar to Hawaii's Waikiki. Rivermouth and Steamer Lane are

SURFING AREAS

CALIFORNIA

SAN FRANCISCO

SANTA CRUZ
CARMEL

RINCON
SANTA BARBARA   COUNTY LINE
(Campus Beach)   MALIBU
VENTURA OVERHEAD   LOS ANGELES
ARROYO SEQUIT   HUNTINGTON BEACH
ZUMA   LAGUNA BEACH
PALOS VERDES   SAN ONOFRE
LA JOLLA-SAN DIEGO
(Wind an' Sea)

TIJUANA SLOUGHS   K-39 (MEXICO)

other favorite areas. Steamer Lane has some of the biggest surf on the California coast. A drive along the Santa Cruz beaches will reveal many surfing spots. Pick your surfing area with care, avoid the rips which form when the surf is up, and from early fall to late spring use a wet suit jacket.

From Santa Cruz to Rincon. There are only a few surfing spots along these three hundred miles of rugged coast. Just south of Santa Cruz and Monterey lies the famous beach of Carmel. Surfers have just begun sliding the waves off Carmel's Seventeen Mile Drive, wearing wet suits, of course. Below Carmel, for the next one hundred and fifty miles to Point Concepcion, the coast is extremely rough and it's almost impossible to reach the beach from a road. There are points where surf breaks but currents are dangerous and the water cold. Below Point Concepcion is Southern California and warmer water. The next good surfing beach, moving south toward Mexico, is Campus Beach at the University of California at Santa Barbara. Campus Beach is a winter surfing spot. North swells of winter are required to start it breaking. Winter waves are not crowded here, but parking is. Only University students and employees can park close enough to reach the beach. Others must walk over from nearby Goleta Beach. Because of the good winter surfing there is talk of making surfing a physical education course at the University.

Rincon. Near the Santa Barbara-Ventura County line is one of California's best point-break surfing areas, the Rincon. The Spanish called it Rincon del Mar, a corner of the sea. Rincon is a north swell break. From November until spring the waves line up with strength and grace and roll in with almost perfect consistency. Rincon has waves up to twelve feet that start feathering and form a shoulder a good half mile from shore. In the 1950's, Rincon was frequented only by a few surfing pioneers. The waves were uncrowded and a surfer could pick and choose, letting many less than perfect waves go by. Now Rincon gets a good weekend crowd, but the early-bird surfer and the weekday rider still find Rincon a surfer's paradise.

From Rincon to Malibu. Driving south from Rincon are several other point and reef breaks. They can be spotted from the coast highway. Sometimes these rarely surfed spots are quite good but they do not have the consistency of Rincon. An alert surfer hunting waves should keep an eye out for any point of land that will start surf breaking. A spot might show surf only a few days out of the year. The watchful surfer can have a good day with only one or two others to share the waves.

The next major spot below Rincon is the Ventura Overhead—called the Overhead because the highway rises to cross over the coast railway tracks. The Overhead, located just beyond the north boundary of the city of Ventura, is a reef break and due to the depth of the reef below the surface a good strong swell is required to start it breaking. When the surf does rise, crest and roll in, the waves are five feet and up. The Overhead can be ridden right or left off the shoulders. Overhead breaks quite far out and the swim back can be very rough if you lose your board. The Overhead is seldom crowded; beginners leave it alone.

County Line, so called because it sits on the Los Angeles-Ventura County border, is also a reef break, but it's quite close to shore and not so hazardous as the Overhead. County Line is great fun, and it breaks in both summer and winter.

Just over the hill from County Line is Leo Carrillo State Beach Park. The local surfers still call it by it's pre-park name—Arroyo Sequit. Sequit is a beautiful little bay that starts breaking as summer swells roll in over a rocky point. Sequit is a high-tide spot because the beach is very rocky. A wipe-out at low tide means a long walk over slippery rocks to the sand.

A few miles below Leo Carrillo-Sequit is the immense stretch of public beach called Zuma. Zuma has plentiful surf, but the waves are mostly shorebreak and ideal for hot-dogging. The lifeguards at Zuma allow surfing until eleven in the morning.

Down the Pacific Coast Highway and around a few curves and past some fancy beach homes is Malibu—the most famous surfing beach in the world except for Waikiki. Since the advent of Hollywood surfing films, Malibu has become the mecca for thousands of new surfers in California. Malibu, on a good summer day when the south swells boom in, can't be beat. It's a beautiful place to surf, and a beginner can learn on the almost perfect waves in a very short time. The waves are splendid for hot-dogging, and when they build to six and seven feet, all sorts of stunts can be performed on their smooth surface. Malibu is best in the early morning before the winds.

From Malibu to Palos Verdes. Going south for the next thirty miles a surf searcher follows the contour of Santa Monica Bay. Within the crescent of the bay are many surfing areas. None are perfect, but many are good with the right conditions. This is the greater Los Angeles surfing area and most spots are crowded. A drive down and around the bay will reveal people surfing wherever a wave builds, even for a few feet. There is good surf at Santa Monica Canyon, Playa del Rey and the beaches of the city towns of Manhattan, Hermosa and Redondo. A check with any of the many local surf shops will provide the visitor with information on where to surf and how to get there.

From Palos Verdes to Mexico. The big deep cove just south of Palos Verdes Estates has been a favorite California surfing spot for thirty years. The bay at Palos Verdes is unchanged since the first hundred-pound redwood board was hand-carried down the long trail to the rocky beach below. This is winter surf, and it can build to fifteen feet and up on good days. A reef about half a mile from shore starts the surf breaking. Right slides or left can be made. The surf is not critical unless it's giant size. Many a surfer made his first stand-up ride at Palos Verdes and most days there is still

Point break, at Malibu's Surfrider Beach on a crowded summer day. The surf is small but consistent, and each wave has a well-formed shoulder. There are nearly a hundred boards in the water at one time.

Dick Gustafson

room for beginners. The surf breaks well at both high and low tide, depending on the height of the swell. It's rather difficult to find the cove. Ask at the only gas station in Palos Verdes Estates for directions, or go about half a mile from the town, where cars are parked along the edge of the road. Look over the edge of the cliff; far below and a long way from shore there will be surfers waiting for a wave. Palos Verdes is good surfing. Try it on a sunny winter morning when the swells are rolling in all the way from Alaska.

South of Los Angeles is Orange County, so named because of orange groves (which have now been replaced by homes). Along the Orange County coast there are dozens of surfing spots. Just below the sprawling city of Long Beach and opposite the rows of pumping oil wells lies the surf of Huntington Beach, which has been called the surf capital of the United States. The five miles of beach stretching north of Huntington Beach Pier produce some of the better waves on the Southern California coast. There are excellent waves on either side of the pier. The annual Huntington Beach surf contest is now a huge competition and crowd drawer. One of the local tricks is to "shoot the pier," which is riding in, through, and out of the concrete barnacle-encrusted pilings.

Below Huntington are several other surfing areas which can be seen from the road. In Laguna Beach there are good surf spots at the ends of Brooks Street and Oak Street. Brooks is high-tide surf and very rocky.

Farther down the highway is Dana Point. This is point surf and quite consistent. It is somewhat crowded in the summer but the gentle break makes it a good area for beginners. There's also good surf below Dana Point off Doheney State Park. The park has facilities for overnight camping. Doheney's surf is gentle and fine for the beginning or intermediate surfer.

Past the city of San Clemente is the old surfer's home beach of San Onofre. San Onofre has been surfed as long as Palos Verdes—perhaps longer. A gradually descending ocean floor combined with an outside reef produces very gentle surf. Even when the waves are ten feet and up the surf is usually manageable. Rips are not a problem, but getting to the beach is. The land around San Onofre is part of a U.S. Marine Corps reservation. The Marines have let the San Onofre surfers form a club, and only club members are allowed to pass over the Marine road to the beach.

Down the coast from San Onofre is the La Jolla-San Diego surfing area. The beach just to the north of La Jolla is attractive, wide and quite surfable. The mile or so of public beach has all the conveniences—clean rest rooms, places to change and even showers—plus good shore surf most of the year. In addition, the lifeguard service, operated by the city of San Diego, is conscious of the surfers' welfare and considers surfing part of the total recreational program. Hats off to San Diego.

Also in the San Diego area is Wind an' Sea (or Windansea), an old California surf spot and still very popular—and crowded. The surf breaks best on a south swell and when the swells generate waves of five feet and up Wind an' Sea is tops. Rides can be made either left or right.

Sunset Cliffs, another San Diego surf spot, is located in the Point Loma area. There is no beach; surfers have to hike down the rock face of the cliffs, toss their boards into the water between waves, then jump in after them. At high tide it's almost impossible to get back to land. Most surfers time their sport so they will finish at low tide.

Below Sunset Cliffs, on the south side of San Diego, near the Mexican border, is the Tijuana Sloughs. There are three breaks: a shorebreak, a middle break, and an outside break. The far break can be as far as a half mile from shore, a long swim if wiped out there. Tijuana Sloughs is for the expert. Local surfers report sharks and killer whales in the area, and dense fogs roll in quick enough to obscure the shore before the surfer can make it back to the beach. The Sloughs is best in winter when swells are northerly or westerly.

Surfing—East Coast USA

From Rhode Island and New York's Long Island to the tip of Florida there is an abundance of ridable surf. The better spots are scattered; some states have only one or two surfing beaches. Florida, where people have been surfing since the 1930's, is the surf center of the East Coast. The big surf on the Atlantic Coast is dependent on storms; during the fall of 1963 a hurricane blew in and ten-foot ridable surf began breaking off Florida and New York beaches.

Florida surfers enjoy warm water year around, though Daytona waters do get cold enough occasionally for wet suit tops. Many of the Florida beaches break because of sandbars; these produce a spilling, rolling type of surf. Most surfers are congregated in and around Miami and Daytona beaches. A recent Jacksonville surf contest drew 2,000-plus spectators. Here are a few of the Florida surfing beaches:

DAYTONA BEACH

Surf can be found at the Pier and Ormond Beach. This is shorebreak with the best waves forming in winter. Waves three feet and up.

NEW SMYRNA

Another shorebreak area, though rides are of 100 yards and more. Larger surf than Daytona.

PORT CANAVERAL (*Canaveral Jetties*)

Surf forms by the Canaveral Pier; excellent when swells are large. A winter surf spot.

The major problem Florida surfers face is the lack of consistency to their waves. The Bahama Islands act as a breakwater and cut off the normal swells coming in from the far Atlantic. Farther up the coast, at the better surf beaches, the swells have a clear path to shore and the surf breaks with more form and consistency, but the water is cold from fall through spring.

Virginia Beach, Virginia, is one of the better surfing areas on the East Coast. At the south end of Virginia Beach is a steel fishing pier. Rides are made on the north side of the pier and away from it, hence a right slide. About 90 miles south of Virginia Beach is Nags Head, North Carolina. Nags Head has quite large and good surf that sometimes builds to ten feet after a storm. Waves break best in later summer and early fall. Then the chill comes.

Delaware, farther up the coast, has some of the best surf in the Middle Atlantic States. The surfing beaches stretch from Indian River Inlet to Ocean City, Maryland, about twenty miles of fine surfing area. This is open coast and receives open sea swells most of the time. The surfing season is April through October; winter is too cold. There are very few surfers in this area, so miles and miles of unsurfed coast await riders. Shifting sandbars make the surf break better in one location one day and better elsewhere on another day, though some areas have a fair degree of consistency. In years to come the Delaware-Maryland area will undoubtedly attract surfers in great numbers.

Long Beach Island and the New Jersey shore offer good surfing. Well-formed waves roll past the Barnegat Light on the South Jersey coast—four or five feet high and quite surfable.

About thirty-five miles out of New York City on the narrow islands off Long Island's south shore is some of the best surf on the East Coast. Here is a stretch of beach cities named Azores, Lido, Jones, Tobay, Gilgo and Cedar. All have surf, and Gilgo seems to have the best. New York's biggest surf comes in from late August through November. Offshore winds plus storms and hurricanes combine to produce strong swells rolling in from the south. The Gulf Stream comes close to Long Island and keeps the water warm from late spring to early fall. With a good storm driving the swells, Long Island surf can build to ten feet or higher. When conditions are right, rides of over 300 yards have been made.

Since 1956, the surfer population of the East Coast has

been expanding, though surfing was done as far back as 1924, when the great Duke Kahanamoku and his brother Dan rode the waves of New Jersey. The East Coast Surfing Championships were held at Gilgo Beach in 1963, drawing some 200 competitors and a crowd of 8,000. Surfers visiting Long Island and seeking information on when and where to surf might check the phone book for the number of John Hannon, who makes surfboards and has the local surf thoroughly discovered. The local beach lifeguards are another source of information, particularly Tom Coburn, a Gilgo Beach lifeguard and owner of Gilgo's Surfboard Rental Shop.

Hawaii

The Hawaiian Islands have justly earned the reputation as the surfing capital of the world. The island of Oahu offers the major surfing activity. There is good surf on the other islands, but the city of Honolulu, with its international airport, draws the majority of surfers. During the summer

SURFING AREAS

OAHU, HAWAIIAN ISLANDS

NORTH

SUNSET
BANZAI
WAIMEA BAY
KAENA POINT
HALEIWA
KAHANA BAY
YOKAHAMA BAY
MAKAHA
MAKAPUU
ALA MOANA
WAIKIKI

months the southern coast of Oahu has the best surf. The waves have traveled long distances from the far South Pacific, and offshore winds from the north make for good surf. The warm waters mean long and pleasant hours on the board. Summer surf in Hawaii is average size, seldom reaching over ten feet.

As fall approaches, the swells change direction and come rolling in from the north. The north swell produces the giant winter surf. Storms originating in the Arctic create swells of gigantic size. The resulting surf on Oahu's north shore is some of the largest in the world. Winter surf in Hawaii is big and tough, strictly for the expert and his big wave board.

Waikiki. During the tourist season Waikiki is too crowded for safe or enjoyable surfing. Most Waikiki surfers are short-term visitors from the mainland with insufficient experience for tackling the crowded waves. But on uncrowded days, Waikiki is the best place in the world for the beginning surfer. There are several spots where the waves break. Over the years they have been given names like Castles, Public Bath Surf, and the Kings and Queens break. The inshore surf is very gentle and often children of five and six are seen riding little boards. Waikiki also hosts outrigger canoes and catamarans. Concessionaires on the beach rent boards and give instruction.

Makaha. Makaha is on the northwest coast of Oahu and because of its exposed position the swells come in from both north and south. Winter is best; the waves build and break farther out producing a well-formed right-slide point surf. Makaha is famous for its annual International Surfing Contest. The beach is wide and sandy, good for body or bellyboard surfing. Makaha is really for experienced surfers, but if it's not crowded and waves are moderate size, the intermediate surfer could start working up to the bigger ones here. Currents and rips are not overly hazardous, but this can change as the surf builds.

Haleiwa. Around Kaena Point lies Haleiwa. Here the

surf is quite consistent. Reefs and rip currents make this area somewhat dangerous when the surf is up. The reef lies just below the surface. When the surf is down, about five or six feet, Haleiwa is a good area for the intermediate surfer to gain experience.

Waimea Bay. Waimea Bay is the favorite surfing beach for the big wave riders and the surf filmmakers. The surf starts breaking when the swells are fifteen feet and up. Waimea is somewhat protected from the weather and sea, and the swells retain good form. There are ridable waves up to thirty feet. The Waimea surfer should be a strong waterman with the right board and plenty of big wave experience.

The Banzai Pipeline. Another favorite of experts and moviemakers, Banzai Pipeline produces some of the wildest wipe-outs in all surfdom. When conditions are perfect and a northwest swell rolls in, the outside reef starts the surf breaking and a long smooth left slide forms. The currents along-

A classic wave. The place is Avalanche, Hawaii. The wave a mile out from shore. This spot is seldom surfed because of its gigantic waves and great distance from shore.

Ron Church

shore are fierce. In fact, the whole Pipeline is hazardous and best left to professionals.

Sunset Beach. About thirty-five miles north of Honolulu, Sunset has enormous surf. When the gigantic north swells come in, it can be quite treacherous. Most surfers feel they have made the big time once they've mastered Sunset. Sunset is a right-slide spot; riding left is not recommended due to a shallow reef area on the side. There's a fast and furious rip current that runs seaward some distance; several surfers have had to be rescued by surfing firemen or air-sea rescue helicopters. Others have drowned in the rip.

Mexico

Mexico offers several excellent surf locations in Baja California and on the mainland. Baja California's best known spot is called, simply, K 39, because the surf builds opposite the 39th kilometer marker on the road. Below K 39 are several other surfing places on the way to Enseñada. From Enseñada south, the roads get progressively worse, but for the alert and venturesome, many other surfing areas await the traveler down Baja's rutty roads.

On the mainland of Mexico, the surf begins to build below the tip of the Baja California Peninsula. On south, the Pacific swells wash into the mainland unobstructed by land. Finding good surf in Mexico really means finding roads to reach the beaches. Perhaps the most accessible surf spot is Mazatlán, with several good surfing beaches. Right in front of the city is the beach of Olas Atlas (the High Waves).

A mile or so north of the city is a rocky point jutting into the Pacific. Depending on the direction of the swell, the point can be surfed on either side. The waters around Mazatlán are warm and blue. Even in January and February the temperature is quite comfortable. One of the joys of surfing at Mazatlán is the civilized living. Good hotels are available and quite cheap. After April, this coastal part of Mexico gets a bit warm.

To the south of Mazatlán are several other good beaches for surfing. Again, reaching them is a problem. There is surf at San Blas and Puerto Vallarta. The latter town has to be reached by air.

Mexico offers great potential for surf exploration, but better take a four-wheel-drive truck, with surfboards strapped atop.

South America

The only place regularly surfed on the western coast of South America is Peru. Below Lima is the famous Club Waikiki at Miraflores. Until recently, Peruvians used the long solid boards with handles mounted on the tail to help surfers shove the heavy boards through the white water. Back in 1950 or so, the founder of the Club Waikiki, Carlos Dogny, visited Malibu and saw surfers using the light, all-balsa boards. The author met Mr. Dogny on the beach and loaned him his balsa board. Very shortly, the first balsas arrived in Peru and the surfing boom began there. There are several other surf areas near Miraflores. As roads and transportation improve, more surfing beaches will be discovered along the great length of the Peruvian and South American coast.

Australia

Australia—country, continent and island—is completely surrounded by water. The miles and miles of coastline are just now feeling the slice of skeg through clear blue water. The first surfer to visit Australia was Duke Kahanamoku, who dazzled the locals back in 1915. Australians have since taken up the sport with great enthusiasm.

Australian surfing centers around Sydney, the country's largest city. Within one hundred miles of Sydney are dozens of good surfing beaches. The famous Fairy Bower on Sydney's north side has fine winter surf that is started breaking by a reef. Bondi Beach and Dee Why Point are other famous Sydney surfing spots. The northern beaches of Queensland have warmer waters which make it quite popular, as well as many excellent surfing beaches. Almost any kind of surf can be found along Australia's eastern coast. There are reef breaks, point breaks, shorebreaks, breaks formed from jetties and sandbar surf. The Sunset Beach of Australia is called the Queen's Cliff Bombora. *Bombora* is an aboriginal term for a type of surf created when winds drive swells over a reef. The Bombora was first ridden in June of 1961, by Australian surfer Dave Jackman. Jackman reported the surf was over twenty feet that day and was breaking over three-quarters of a mile out.

Australia produces an abundance of fine surf and friendly surfers. Sportsmanship is valued and practiced, and the tradition of the volunteer lifesaving clubs has been taken up by surfers. There is one disadvantage to surfing in Australia— sharks. Australia has more shark incidents than any other country. During the shark's mating season, which is our winter months and their summer season, the danger from shark attack is great. On the public beaches many measures are taken to protect bathers, but surfers riding at isolated beaches are on their own.

Australia does have a problem with crowded waves in and around the large metropolitan areas but a drive of a few miles will take one to perfect waves and unspoiled beaches.°

New Zealand

East of Australia lies the twin island nation of New Zealand. Here are miles of beaches that seldom see a swimmer and hardly ever a surfer. Right out of the capital city of Auckland is a beach called Takapuna where the surf breaks well and during winter storms forms a five- to six-foot right slide. North of Auckland are other surfing areas. New

° For additional details on Australian surfing see: *The Australian Surfrider* by Jack Pollard. K. G. Murry Publishing Company, Ltd., Sydney, Australia.

Zealand has no shark problem, the waves are uncrowded and there is beautiful scenery everywhere. One drawback is the cold water. Winter surfing on the more exposed west coast is definitely wet-suit water; the water temperatures drop as low as 48° to 58°. The eastern coastal water is slightly warmer, reaching a chilly height of 64°. The Takapuna Surf Club out of Auckland will provide surfing information, as will the Auckland Chamber of Commerce. In 1963, New Zealand held its first Surfing Championships and the sport appears to be well on the way to popularity. For the surfer looking for waves that have never been ridden, it's New Zealand—before the crowds.

South Africa

The center of South African surfing is in and around Cape Town and Durban. Cape Town faces the Antarctic and is blessed with swells from both the Atlantic and Indian oceans. Surfing beaches lie along the South African coast from Cape Town to Durban, a distance of approximately 1,200 miles. Durban is on the Indian Ocean side of South Africa. The waters of Cape Town are like California waters —fairly warm in summer (*their* summer) and chilly in winter. Durban has tropic waters with temperatures ranging up to the low eighties. The long South African coastline provides plenty of room for surfers—and sharks. The warmer waters around Durban attract large numbers of sharks and local surfers team up to surf. One watches for dorsal fins while the other rides.

Within twenty-five miles of Cape Town are several excellent beaches for surfing. To the east of the city is a surf area known as Muizemberg (or Mouse in the Mountain). The surf here rolls in with nice even lines. One of Cape Town's favorite surfing spots is called The Pipe. This spot was formed when a freighter sank and provided an artificial reef for the surf to build on. Check with the lifeguards at

Cape Town public beaches for surf information and whom to contact for a possible surfing companion.

France

On the west coast of France, exposed to the long swells from the South Atlantic, surfing has come of age for the French. The Bay of Biscay is the center of French surfing and the coastal resort city of Biarritz is surfing headquarters. Back in 1957 the American writer Peter Viertel was in France working on the film version of Hemingway's *The Sun Also Rises*. While at Biarritz, Mr. Viertel saw the possibilities of the French surf and had a balsa board shipped in from California. The French, being very sports-minded, saw the fun and thrills of surfing and went all out to get surfing started in their country. Several years later there were hundreds of surfers and the surf scene had expanded into Spain.

The months between September and November and April and May are best. Summer surf is good, but not as large or consistent. During the surf season waves as large as fifteen feet rise off the better beaches within the Bay of Biscay. North Atlantic waters are cold and French waters are no exception. In the spring and fall the temperature is in the mid-fifties, rising to 70° in the summer. Surfers going to France will find French wave riders good companions. Bill Cleary, a well-traveled surfer and editor of *Surf-Guide* magazine, has ridden French waves; surfers wishing additional information can write to Cleary in care of the magazine.

Chapter 14

THE MODERN SURFBOARD

MOST surfboards have the same general appearance, and it's hard to tell one from the other. Like a golf club or bowling ball the surfboard conforms to a single design. It's only with a closer look that the differences emerge. The expert bowler, golfer, or skier spends a great deal of time on the finer details of his equipment, and so do expert surfers.

A well-made surfboard is both functional and eye pleasing. The curve of the rails, the balance of line and form, and the smooth, often colorful covering all speak of something that was made to be swift and graceful.

Surfboards have evolved from the old Hawaiian solid-carved-from-tree-trunk boards to redwood and pine giants, to long thin teardrop-shaped hollow designs, to blunt-nose and -tail balsas, to a variety of shapes achieved through the bonding of fiberglass to polyurethane foam. Since surfing is a very individualistic sport, the types of boards built over the years have reflected every possible type of personal innovation. Someone is always thinking about a new design concept, investing in materials, and launching through the surf ready to prove he has "the answer." Boards have been built that collapse in three pieces to fit in suitcases. Hollow shells of fiberglass weighing ten pounds have been tried. Boards

Pete Peterson, "Surfing's Iron Man," riding an old, solid redwood board straight off an unbroken swell. Over the past thirty years Preston Peterson has won more surfing contests than any other person. Photograph taken during the 1940s when wooden boards were used.

have been covered with floral-patterned fiberglass window curtains. And several people have tried building boards with a double bottom that was supposed to raise them up on a hydrofoil once sufficient speed was obtained. All these ideas worked to a limited extent, but none has replaced the basic design concept of the artfully rounded nose and the slight taper to a rounded or nearly square tail.

Other innovations in board building are the double and triple skeg, the skeg that looks like a croquet wicket (called a tunnel skeg), and even a board with a speedometer. Some boards are made so they will turn faster to left or right. Some of the heavy old-timers had handles built in for carrying and one was made with a silver dollar molded into the nose so the surfer would never be broke. One surfer even had a color photograph of a painting of a Roman bacchanal molded under the fiberglass and named his board The Orgy.

In general three basic types of boards have evolved from the years of experimentation: The hot dog or hot curl board, the big gun board, and the Malibu board. These three types are produced with great variation in shape, weight, length, thickness, and covering. Yet even with this variation they can be categorized into the three basic shapes.

The Hot Dog Board. Identifiable by short length, deep skeg, and a broad surface area at the tail, the hot dog board is designed to perform well in fast-breaking surf of small to medium size. Because of the deep skeg that is set as far back as possible, the hot dog board will turn rapidly and permit the rider to work the board all over the face of a wave. The broad tail, when it's kept in the break, holds well and aids the surfer as he moves forward. The hot dog board rarely runs over nine feet and a few inches depending on the size and weight of the individual surfer. Generally the smaller boards don't paddle well and are harder to pick up a wave on unless the face of the wave is steep. But for riding fast shorebreak they are ideal. A bigger, slower-turning board just won't bust out of a wipe out wave fast enough. Some of the early hot dog boards were called pig boards because of their fat rear end. The normal hot dog board has fairly full edges, flat top and bottom and a slight lift or rocker toward the nose. The hot dog board is not a good choice for beginners because it is just too specialized and hard to handle.

The Big Guns. Used for heavy surf, the big guns came into being about 1949. Joe Quigg, one of the early California board builders, constructed the first of the big gun breed. Quigg built it for one of the pioneer big-wave riders, Buzzy Trent. The board was about 12 feet long and 20 inches wide, extremely long and narrow by more modern standards. The long, needle-shaped board was almost too fast. It raced away from the break before the owner really had time to enjoy the wave. Big gun boards were modified until a compromise design finally evolved. Recent big-wave boards are around 11 feet long, 22 inches wide, 4 inches thick, and combine features that permit both speed and control. The long big-wave board is quite heavy compared with the hot dog and Malibu board. It often runs up to 40 pounds, the weight being necessary to keep the board stable and under control on a fast slide across a wind-chopped 20-foot comber. The bottom of the big-wave board is quite rounded toward the nose. This rounded portion, called the crown, helps stabilize the board when it drops down the front of a wave in choppy water. On flat-bottomed boards there is a tendency for the nose portion to slap and chatter when sliding over rough water.

Younger surfers like the idea of having a "gun" board. It's a status symbol, but since big waves are not the general rule but the hope of most surfers, a big gun is impractical. The baby gun or semi-gun was developed because surfers wanted a board that could be used in big surf as well as in normal waves. This is a shorter board but still tapering toward the tail and rounded under the nose. The semi-guns are about 10 feet long. California and Eastern United States surf doesn't build to good size frequently enough to justify even a semi-gun surfboard.

It's a different matter in the Hawaiian Islands. Year-round Hawaiian surfers usually own two boards, one for normal-size waves and a big gun for the heavies.

The shorter semi-gun boards are not as fast, but they are more maneuverable and you can do a bit of big-wave hot-dogging on them. Because of their lack of speed in big surf, the semi-gun boards (like the Malibu boards) must be ridden closer to the top of the wave. This is due to the board's tendency to climb when put into a critical angle. A real big gun board should make a clean drop down the face of the wave after the takeoff, accelerate quickly, and be able to trim easily.

An interesting test of how true a board is in shape and symmetry is the chatter effect. If the skeg is not in line or precisely in the center, and if the bottom is uneven, the board tends to hum or chatter when going fast. Some boards pound and shake and others seem to pull slightly right or left. Good board design overcomes this; most custom builders make sure that skegs and rails are true. In the days when boards were homemade or entirely shaped by eye the chatter effect was quite common.

The Malibu Board. Sometimes called a beach board, the Malibu is the best all-around piece of surfing equipment developed so far. The Malibu shape is a compromise between the guns and the hot-dogging boards.

One personality in the surfing world stands out in the development of modern surfboards and is almost a legend now. This is the late Bob Simmons who more than anyone else brought the Malibu board and modern surfing to their present eminence. Due to an early injury Bob Simmons partially lost the use of his left arm. The disability made it hard for Bob to lug around the heavy surfboards of the 1940's and early 1950's. Bob developed several prototypes of the current Malibu board, and each version was a bit lighter and more suitable for the California surf he used to ride and like so well. Some authorities claim Bob was the first to build an

These boards, owned by the author, represent a thirty-year history of surfing. The board on the left is a modern foam and fiberglass design, the center board a classic paddleboard, and at right an early *Malibu* type built around 1946.

all-balsawood board, but not so. Preston "Pete" Peterson built several varnish-covered balsas during the 1930's, but this was before fiberglass. What Simmons did that was so important was to perfect the application of fiberglass to balsa and design a shape that still endures though modified.

Almost all general-purpose surfboards built today are an

evolution of Simmons' basic design. He came up with such innovations as the bowed shape or rocker, foam sandwiched between thin plywood and covered with glass, deep skeg, and broad tail for rapid turns.

Matt Kivlin of Santa Monica, California, was one of the first to begin producing surfboards commercially. Matt, now a home builder, used to carve out his balsas on the beach until the windblown shavings created a public nuisance. He then rented a shop and the modern one-man custom surfboard factory was born. Matt was also one of the first to use polyurethane foam in board construction, as were Dave Sweet of Santa Monica and Hobi Alter of San Clemente, California, both of whom are still prominent names in the surfboard business.

The Malibu board received its name for obvious reasons: Malibu is where it was first extensively ridden and is one of California's oldest and best surfing spots. Surfers of fame all hold a warm spot in their memories for Malibu. During the balsaboard days such experts as Buzzy Trent, Peter Cole, and Tom Zahn began their surfing careers there. Peter Lawford used to be one of the regulars and old-timers wearing bookkeeper eye shades slid the Malibu break frequently. All this has changed—today the beach is for young people and experts. The boards are almost the same, but surfers grow up and go on. There is a new generation always ready to replace the old, and they quite easily forget that a nice guy with a bad arm gave them all so much. Those who remember Simmons felt a great sadness when the news of his drowning at Wind and Sea spread along the beaches back in 1955.

Modern Surfboard Manufacturing

Foam has almost completely replaced other materials used in surfboard construction. Polyurethane foam has many advantages: light weight, strength, compatability with polyester resins and fiberglass, and low water absorption. Perhaps the most important advantage in manufacturing is that foam can be mixed and molded into almost any size and shape. Surfboards do not come out of the molds as a finished product. Molding the blank is just the first step. The blank is the semi-finished shape that emerges from the mold when the chemicals are mixed and then "cooked." (It is actually the chemical industry that has made the production of foam and glass surfboards possible.) Several chemical ingredients go into the mix before a board blank is cast. The chemical liquids are first heated, mixed in new clean paper containers that can only be used once, and then poured into the molds. (One foam blank manufacturer used so many paper containers that he had to build his own container factory to keep up with his needs.) Once the mix is in the molds it is baked for approximately thirty minutes. The heat cures the foam, which is then removed from the molds. The molded blanks are now ready to be sold to custom shops for final shaping and glassing. Most of these blanks are made oversize so the custom builder can trim them down to shapes desired by individual buyers.

Another way of forming blanks is to create the board right in the mold. In this method the fiberglass covering is molded first and then the plastic foam is allowed to cure inside. This is the least expensive way. There are several disadvantages to this method of construction. The glass doesn't bond well to the foam and may blister if left in the sun. The skeg cannot be fixed firmly to the fiberglass, and the seam or joint where the two halves are joined together is not sufficiently strong. Mass-produced boards have not as yet matched the quality of the custom-made product. Though factory models are cheaper, inferior quality tells in the long run. As the mass producers gain experience, their product will likely improve.

Custom shops still dominate the surfboard market. The man who owns his own shop and whose livelihood depends on building a good product makes sure his board is first

Con Surfboards

Inserting a redwood stringer between the split foam blank. The blank at this point is oversize. Later it will be shaped to the desired specifications.

quality. The builder of custom boards normally buys molded blanks, called shaping blanks, from a foam manufacturer. The market for the unfinished blanks is quite astounding. A few years ago builders carved a few hundred boards a year from balsa. Recently production has jumped to 15,000 to 20,000 boards per year in Southern California alone. Combine this estimate with the boards produced in Hawaii, Australia and the one or two shops in France and Peru and that's a lot of surfboards. If the average surfboard from a custom shop costs $100 and 15,000 are sold annually, the gross in the surfboard market jumps to an astounding $1,500,000.

Building the Custom Board

Most custom shops build boards in the slow, sure, all-by-hand method. The basic foam blanks are purchased in

wholesale quantities from several plastic foam manufacturers. The blanks are oversized and quite crude-looking at
first.

After the blanks reach the custom shop they are sawed in
half. Next a wooden stringer is placed between the two
halves, glue is smeared on, and the board is placed in clamps
to set the glue and dry. The customer may choose any one
of several combinations of wood stringers. The stringer gives
the board longitudinal strength. A ten-foot hunk of lightweight foam without the stiffener just doesn't have the
strength to take the pounding of the surf and the crash
against sand or rocks. Some surfers will choose such combinations of stringers as pine-redwood-pine, or a two-inch
strip of balsa, or even five half-inch strips of ash separated
by an inch or more of foam. These special orders cost considerably more, but they do add an individual touch and
help identify the board.

After the blank and stringer are released from the gluing
clamps the custom shaper picks up his power plane and begins to work. The revolving blades of the plane cut through
the foam and wood, chipping away toward the eventual
shape specified by the customer. When the power plane
work is finished the shaper's eyes and rough sandpaper in
conjunction give the nearly finished blank its final shape.
The builder's skill pays off here. He will sight down the rails
and across the white surfaces again and again as he sands a
bit here and there. At last he is satisfied that the board is
shaped to the customer's specifications and the time has arrived to commit the board to its covering of fiberglass.

The fiberglassing of a surfboard is a sticky, messy business
requiring great care and precision. If the glass job is not
right all the work of the shaper will have been wasted. The
glass covering adds great strength to the board and protects
the foam from the rotting and weight-increasing effects of
salt water.

There are three major phases to glassing a board: (1) the

lamination of the glass cloth and resin to the foam blank; (2) the setting of the skeg to the tail; and (3) the final gloss and color (if color is being used) coat. Fiberglassing is explained in more detail in the chapter on building a board. Most strongly built boards have the glass covering overlapping on the rails so there is a double thickness for strength. The rails, nose, and tail take the roughest treatment during a board's surfing life.

Dave Sweet, one of the early California custom surfboard makers, has developed a secret compromise between the factory product and the hand-built board. Dave has invented an adjustable mold for "blowing" his own foam blanks. He has some fifty different molds (the exact number is his own trade secret). Each mold can be adjusted to produce a variety of shapes within certain limitations. The fine adjustments enable boards to be molded very close to the customer's specifications. With the large number of molds and the adjustable feature it is mathematically possible to produce over 5,000 different shapes of surfboards. The blanks come from the molds so perfectly finished that very little handwork is required to prepare them for fiberglassing.

Not all boards are made to individual specifications. Builders keep standard sizes in stock. Competition among builders is fierce. New techniques and gimmicks are constantly devised to attract customers. Successful builders run full-page advertisements in the surfing magazines and have developed a mail order business. It is safe to order a board by mail from a recognized surfboard shop. The following shops have been in business for some time and produce quality boards.

MAJOR CUSTOM SURFBOARD BUILDERS

Bing Surfboards	1820 Pacific Coast Hwy.
	Hermosa Beach, California
Con Surfboards	824 Pico Blvd.
	Santa Monica, California

MAJOR CUSTOM SURFBOARD BUILDERS (Continued)

Diwain Surfboards	134 S. Pacific Avenue
	Redondo Beach, California
Greg Noll Surf Boards	1402 Pacific Coast Hwy.
	Hermosa Beach, California
Hobie Surfboards	34195 Pacific Coast Hwy.
	Dana Point, California
Hobie Surfboards	Hawaii
	1475 Kapiolana, Honolulu
Hobie Surfboards	Peru
	Luis Cabllero Vagas
	Malecon Balta 934, Miraflores, Lima
	Also through distributors in
	New York, New Jersey, Virginia
	and Florida.
Jacobs Surfboards	422 Pacific Coast Hwy.
	Hermosa Beach, California
Dave Sweet Surfboards	1408 Olympic Blvd.
	Santa Monica, California
Dewey Weber Surfboards	4116 Lincoln Blvd.
	Santa Monica, California
West Coast East Surf Shop	137 Fifth Street
	Miami, Florida
Wardy Surfboards	806 East Colorado Blvd.
	Pasadena, California
Santa Barbara Surf Shop	Lillie Ave.
	Summerland, California
Gordon Woods Surfboards	208 Harbord Road
	Sydney, Australia
Surfboards Hawaii	66-479 Kamehameha Hwy.
	P. O. Box 1, Haleiwa, Hawaii

Prices of custom-made boards do not vary greatly; $100 is a good starting figure. Prices go up depending on size and complexity of the stringer layout and color scheme. A very special ten-foot job with several stringers and a complex color layout might cost close to $200. The extra stringers and special color designs are just frosting on the board. If the board is a good basic shape, the glass laid on properly, and the skeg set firmly, then only one ¾-inch stringer is necessary. The owner can add color himself by mixing his own resin and color, saving several dollars. When ordering by mail the customer should specify his size and weight and the type of surf he usually would expect to ride. Get a firm price quotation from the builder before sending a check. Figure on shipping charges too, and don't forget the thirty-five cents for a package of paraffin to wax the board with—that's about all the upkeep a good board will need.

Boards are sold by the factory mass producers through the mails and through distributors. Many companies have grown up overnight with the surfing boom. If your local dealer will guarantee the board and you know the distributor is in business to stay, it might be safe to purchase a mass-produced board from him. Make sure the agreement with the seller includes a return if the board bulges and the glass separates from the foam when it sits in the sun and heats.

In buying surfboards you get what you pay for. Buying from a recognized builder will insure a quality board that will last and perform as it was designed to.

What Is a Good Board?

There are over forty surfboard shops in business. Each custom shop builds a board slightly differently—different in shape, materials and quality. The following are a few ideas of what constitutes a good board.

The heart of a sound board is the foam. The stronger and denser the foam the sturdier the board will be. In selecting a board try to find one that contains a good hard foam. Hard foams are more difficult to shape and don't lend themselves to mass-production techniques. Foam manufactured by one of the three or four recognized molders of blanks will usually be of good quality.

Choose a board with a good solid stringer. The stringer gives the board good lateral strength and keeps the pitch or rocker from warping. Stringers that are inlaid, that don't go all the way through the foam core, are probably not as strong as a solid strip of wood, though good-quality fiberglassing will make up for this. Extra stringers may add some strength but they also add weight. One good stringer will do the job.

The skeg is very important, and a skeg that is not secured properly to the tail of the board will break in time. Skegs are made of many materials; wood, foam covered with glass, plexiglass, nylon and metal have all been used. Probably the most practical fin material in use today is the all-fiberglass skeg. The solid glass skeg bonds well, resists impact and is very strong. Glass fins that have chipped or have large nicks in them can be sanded down, given a coat of resin and plopped back in the surf with little time lost. The beaded wooden fins are quite attractive, but they don't hold up as well. The fin should have a substantial ridge built up around the base to give it strength. When a fin comes off it's a major repair to put back on. Let an expert make the repair, watch him if possible and do it yourself if there's a next time.

A good fiberglass covering for the board should be smooth, free from any rough spots and dense enough to offer protection from most impacts. The glass can be double coated if the extra cost isn't a problem, or the glass can be heavier and one coat used. Ten- and twenty-ounce cloth is the standard weight used in board building. Most surfers like to have a double layer of ten-ounce cloth; they feel this is the best combination for strength. In any case the glass should be double wrapped over the rails. The overlap should extend over the rails and onto the flat surface of the bottom and the deck.

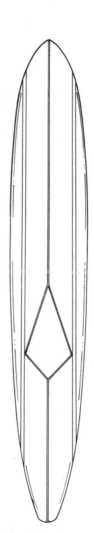

This redwood-balsa board grew to eleven feet or so and often weighed close to a hundred pounds. Used extensively up to 1948.

The Simmons shape, first to use foam and fiberglass for buoyancy and a watertight c o v e r-ing. Shape is old style but weight was cut almost in half.

"Pig board," one of the first hot dog types. Balsa wood covered with fiber-glass. Popular in the early 1950s.

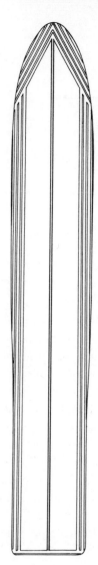

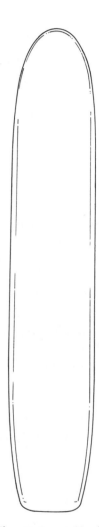

Current *M a l i b u* or beach board shape. The standard design of most m o d e r n boards. Foam and glass cloth. Seldom over thirty-five pounds.

The semi-gun. Used for m e d i u m to large surf.

The big gun. Almost eleven and a half feet, weighs c l o s e to fifty pounds. Designed for speed and stability on the Hawaiian heavy surf.

Chapter 15

BUILDING A SURFBOARD

UNTIL recently most surfboards were handmade by the people who rode them. As far back as the 1930's building a surfboard or paddleboard was one of the standard high school woodshop projects in Southern California schools. Surfboard building techniques have changed since the days of gluing redwood or balsa together, slapping on several coats of varnish and rooting in the skeg. The modern surfboard is considerably more complex in design and fabrication than its wooden forefather. Foam and fiberglass aren't as available as wood and glue yet and the technique of laminating fiberglass to foam is a relatively new process. Even with these limitations it's still possible for the backyard craftsman to construct his own board. With careful workmanship and attention to detail the end result can be very satisfactory.

One of the major problems of home surfboard construction is acquiring all the materials. Most smaller communities don't have stores that carry large stocks of foam or even fiberglass and resin. However, this problem can be overcome. Today surfboard kits are available and come complete with all the necessary materials and instructions. There are also preshaped foam blanks that can be purchased directly from the manufacturer. The basic foam core can be obtained in a kit as a preshaped board ready to glass, from a foam blank manufacturer already shaped, with or without wooden stringer, or from a plastics fabricator as a solid rectangular piece of foam. By far the best and easiest way to build a board is to start with a blank that is preshaped; either from a blank builder or in kit form. If the home builder chooses to design his own shape, the solid plank of foam will have to be used. We won't consider building a board from a foam plank here. The construction of the precision templates needed to form the exact curves is beyond the scope of this chapter.* For an example, we'll use either a factory-blown blank or the foam blank that comes out of the kit. Once the preshaped blank is acquired the next steps are about the same for either type of foam blank.

The Foam Core

In general, foam blanks come in two types. The most common is the shaping foam blank which is made oversize so the builder can create his own variation in width, thickness, length, rocker and weight. Shaping blanks can be purchased with the wood stringer already glued in. The other type is the hard shell blank which has the final shape created in the mold. These preshaped blanks sometimes have a thin paper shell left over from the molding process. This paper covering should remain, but it can be roughened by sanding for a better bond between blank and fiberglass. The kit board blanks are of this variety. In general the higher the foam density, the stronger the surfboard will be. There are several major foam blank manufacturers and one kit board company at this time. More companies will undoubtedly spring up as the number of customers increase. Here are the companies:

The Foss Company
1763 Placentia Avenue
Costa Mesa, California

* Detailed instructions on building from the foam plank can be obtained from: *The Surfboard Builder's Manual*, by Steve Shaw, Products Unlimited, La Mesa, California, $3.00. This publication shows how to construct templates and gives additional details for the noncommercial builder.

Dave Sweet Surfboards (will ship anywhere)
1408 Olympic Boulevard
Santa Monica, California

H. Walker Company
1315 North El Camino Real
San Clemente, California

For kit boards:

Plastic Mart (for both wave and wake surfing kits)
1710 Colorado Avenue
Santa Monica, California

All of the above companies have been in business some years and have good reputations. A letter sent to any one of them should bring a quote on prices and delivery times. Anyone looking for a foam blank could also contact his local surfboard shop for additional information.

Fiberglass

Fiberglass cloth starts its life as glass marbles. The marbles are melted and the molten glass is forced through tiny orifices and the filaments are twisted into a strand as they emerge. After being coated with a starchlike compound they can be handled like ordinary cotton cloth and can be woven with standard textile machinery. The individual fiberglass strand may be only one-fifteenth the diameter of a human hair.

Fiberglass used for surfboard covering should be finished with volan chrome or a similar chemical to insure that the resin will bond to the glass cloth. Boards can be single or double coated with glass. For single coating use 16-ounce to 20-ounce weight glass; for double coating 8½- to 13-ounce glass cloth should be used. Most board builders use 10-ounce cloth for a double coating and 20-ounce for a single covering. Many boating supply houses sell glass and resin suitable

BUILDING A SURFBOARD 195

for covering the board. Chemical supply houses could also furnish resin and glass cloth as well as provide further information on their own products.

Resin and Catalyst

In order to achieve a permanent bond of fiberglass to foam, a mixture of polyester or isopthalic resins and a catalyst is used to harden and laminate the glass and resin. Only a few drops of catalyst is required to start the reaction which causes the resin to harden. It is extremely important to follow the manufacturer's instructions when mixing resin and catalyst. A drop or two extra might cause the resin to jell faster than it can be applied. A spoonful of extra catalyst will produce a resin mix so "hot" it will smoke and cure very fast. A great deal of catalyst can result in a violent chemical reaction, such as an explosion or fire. The curing time of catalyzed resin will also be affected by the temperature and exposure of the resin to ultraviolet rays, i.e., sunlight. When purchasing resins, insist on the best quality available. There are no discounts on good-quality resin.

Construction Techniques

If the home surfboard builder is working from a kit, all the instructions and materials will be provided by the manufacturer. If he's starting with a shaping blank or a preshaped and molded blank, the following description will serve as a general guide for building the board.

Before starting, be sure to have all the materials and tools on hand. The want of a few pieces of sandpaper might slow up the job and keep the board out of the water the one extra day when the surf is "up." Another important consideration before starting is to find a good place to work. The workshop should be well ventilated and free from dust as well as have enough room for the builder to move around the board. In addition there should be a good workbench to place the board on or a sturdy pair of padded sawhorses. Wherever the board is placed, the surface it lies on should be padded so the foam will not be gouged by sharp edges.

TOOLS AND SUPPLIES

Sandpaper: At least ten sheets each of course and medium open coat garnet paper.

Electric Sander: The heavy-duty orbital types work best. Circular sanders can dig in and belt sanders cut too fast when working on the rails, nose or tail. Have plenty of sandpaper.

Sanding Block: Makes hand sanding easier and helps produce a smooth cut.

Safety Razor Blade or X-Acto Knife: Used to trim fiberglass after resin has jelled.

Scissors or Shears: To cut fiberglass, should be heavy-duty type.

Rags: Lots of clean ones to wipe hands, clean up spilled resin, etc.

Mixing Containers: Acquire clean paper pails or save old coffee cans and make sure they are clean. Used for mixing catalyst and resin. Don't forget clean sticks to stir with.

Paintbrushes: One 3" or 4" and one 2". Use pure bristles; the chemicals will affect nylon bristles.

Acetone (1 gal.): Used to clean brushes, hands and spilled resin.

Masking Tape: 2 large rolls of 2-inch tape.

Squeegees, 2 or 3: Used to spread resin and force liquid into fiberglass. Can be handmade from stiff cardboard.

Dust Cloth or Feather Duster: Used to brush away sanded fiberglass particles.

Shopcoat or Long-sleeve Shirt: Sanded fiberglass can cause a skin itch. Keep as much of it as possible off the skin.

MATERIALS

Foam Surfboard Blank:

Glass Cloth: Purchase enough to extend over the nose and tail by four to six inches and over the widest part of the board by four to six inches. You'll need double this amount for both sides.

MATERIALS (*Continued*)

Glass Rope: Used for running a bead around the base of the
   skeg. Two feet would be plenty.
The Skeg: Purchase a fiberglass skeg or make one from wood.
   Copy shape from other boards, or photographs.
Resin (laminating type):   Four quarts.
Resin (glossing and sanding type):   Three quarts.
Catalyst: Two ounces or more, depending on manufacturer's
   instructions.
Color Pigment (if desired):   Follow manufacturer's recommen-
   dations.

And one last item: TIME. Schedule enough time so there
won't be any interruptions, especially when applying the
resin to the glass cloth.

To begin, let's assume the foam blank is in the same general shape that the final board will take and the stringer is
already glued in. If the blank needs further shaping to round
the rails or shorten length, then work slowly and carefully
with coarse sandpaper. When working on the rails, hold the
paper firmly and make long end-to-end sanding strokes. Always keep a careful eye on the area being sanded and check
to see that the rails are kept rounded. Excessive sanding in
one area will quickly result in depressed or out-of-round
areas.

When rough sanding is done switch to a medium grit of
sandpaper. The paper should be backed with a sanding
block for more even cutting. During the final sanding don't
gouge or deep-scratch the foam; this will result in the resin
pooling in the depressions. When the board appears to be
completely sanded and ready for glassing, make one more
detailed check for smooth lines. This is the last opportunity,
for now the final shape will be set in the fiberglass covering.

Fiberglassing

Before starting to glass the board make sure all the materials are assembled. Read the directions on the cans of resin

or any instructions supplied by the manufacturer. Study and understand the ratios of catalyst to resin to be used. A small test batch of resin and catalyst may be mixed to see if the hardening time corresponds to that specified. When all is ready give the blank a final dusting. The sanded foam particles can be blown off by swinging the duster over the board or they can be vacuumed off.

We'll take the top side first. Take the glass cloth and lay it over the board, making sure all the wrinkles are smoothed out. If two layers of glass are being used place the second sheet over the first and again remove wrinkles. Now the excess glass may be cut away. With scissors or shears cut the cloth the same shape as the board, but leave five to seven inches of overhang. Again smooth out wrinkles. Now take the masking tape and apply a piece at the midpoint of the board on both sides. Keep placing tape hold-downs around the rails of the board. When working around the nose or tail, small splits may be made in the cloth to help it make a tight bend. Overlap the cloth where split. When the tape hold-downs are in place make another check for wrinkles. A continuous piece of tape may now be placed around the entire length of the board. This piece lets the excess resin drip straight down and keeps the saturation line even. Later, when the resin has jelled, but not hardened, the cloth behind the tape is cut with a razor or X-Acto knife and the tape is pulled away. This leaves a nice smooth edge.

The Resin Step

If the glass is free of wrinkles, it's time to put on the laminating coat of resin. The resin should be mixed with the catalyst so drying time is not less than thirty minutes. Higher temperatures and sunlight will speed the drying time, so take this into consideration.

Into a clean container, mix a quart and one half of resin. Add the required amount of catalyst. This will be enough to do the top side. Stir the mix thoroughly, but not so vigorously that bubbles form. When the resin is mixed pour about half the batch along the center line of the board. Resin is thick and it will flow slowly toward the rails. Now take the squeegee and work the resin toward the rails and into the cloth. Use a gentle pressure with the squeegee; too much pressure will move the cloth and perhaps cause bubbles. When the cloth has absorbed this application of resin take the remainder and pour it on the dry spots and work in with the squeegee. Some resin will drip off the sides. This is normal and can't be helped if an even smooth coat is to be obtained. If bubbles do form under the cloth try to gently pat

The catalized resin has just been poured and the builder saturates the glass cloth as he spreads the liquid with a rubber squeegee.

Allan Walker

them out. If they can't be removed this way a small slit may be made in the cloth with a razor blade and the air released. When the laminating coat looks smooth, stand back. Don't stir up any dust and let it jell. At this point clean the hands before the resin has a chance to dry. Acetone will cut it but don't use too much as it's very drying to the skin and the fumes are somewhat poisonous if used in an unventilated room.

Just before the glass/resin hardens take a razor blade and trim the cloth along the saturation line. Pull away the tape. Remember the cloth is cut under the top rail. Now wait for the first coat to harden. When the glass/resin is completely hard turn the board over and sand the edges. The sanding should smooth the edges but not cut into the unglassed foam. This is sometimes called feathering the edge. It frequently takes an hour or longer before the resin has hardened sufficiently to sand.

For the bottom side the application of resin to glass is the same. Remember about wrinkles and the need to saturate the cloth completely. As soon as the bottom is done the skeg can be set to the tail.

Applying the Skeg

The skeg must be fastened exactly in the center of the board and set so it leans neither left nor right. If the skeg is set off center the board will not ride true. The skeg may be rooted in or just glassed (a butt joint) to the board. It's a lot easier just to glass the skeg to the center strip and this method is almost as strong as rooting in. A simple way to butt-joint the skeg to the board is to drive some small finishing nails into the bottom of the skeg, gently tap the top of the skeg and drive the nails into the stringer. If the heads of the nails are clipped off first they can be tapped into the skeg. Now the skeg will stand up. Check the angle of the skeg with a level or a right angle. To permanently set the skeg, the bottom edge, which is butted to the stringer, can be fastened with resin and fiberglass rope. Take two pieces of glass rope just slightly longer than the base of the skeg and unwind them slightly. This helps the resin saturate the rope. Next, lay the rope in a can of resin mixed with catalyst. When it is saturated place the rope around the bottom edge of the skeg. To help the resin penetrate the rope it will have to be worked in with the fingers. Now allow the resin-saturated rope to cure and become hard.

After the rope is hardened, sand all the rough strands smooth. Sandpaper wrapped around a dowel helps here. The sanding should produce a smooth surface that tapes so the coming covering of fiberglass will lie up against the skeg and surface of the board. If a wooden skeg is being used, the wood will have to be covered with fiberglass. If a glass skeg is being used, only the bottom half need be covered. In both cases the glass should extend from the bottom of the skeg outward to wrap around the rails. The fiberglass skeg is by far the best material to use.

If a wooden skeg is used, it is sometimes best to create a fiberglass bead to protect the leading edge of the wood. To build the bead, cut out four pieces of glass the shape of the skeg but make them about three inches larger overall. Glass these to the side of the skeg but leave the extra portion which sticks up beyond the top of the skeg dry. Next, cut enough strands of glass rope to fit along the edge of the whole skeg. The rope is unraveled and then saturated with resin and placed between the glass which extends beyond the edge of the skeg. If necessary add more resin with a brush to saturate all the rope and glass along the edge. It may also be necessary to work out the bubbles with the fingers. As the material begins to jell, work the bead with the fingers to a tapered edge. Just before the glass and rope harden, trim the edge to the desired size and let harden.

Now the board is completely covered with fiberglass and ready for the final sanding and the gloss coat of resin. A careful pre-gloss-coat sanding can make the difference be-

Taping on the skeg prior to laying on the first coat of glass cloth. Skeg must be set true so board will function properly. Later the edges of the skeg will be ground and sanded down to a taper.

Allan Walker

The clear gloss coat is being poured on the almost-finished board. In background builder quickly spreads resin with clean bristle brush. Note how smooth the skeg was sanded and how the weave of the glass cloth can be seen.

Allan Walker

tween just another home-built surfboard and a beautiful piece of work. Sanding accomplishes two purposes. It smooths down the rough edges and bits of sharp fiberglass which always seem to occur, and roughs the surface so the gloss coat of resin will adhere well.

The flat surfaces on top and bottom may be machine-sanded but the rails, nose, and tail should be hand-sanded. In any case don't sand through the fiberglass. All bright or shiny areas should be sanded as well. Long smooth strokes are best when hand-sanding. Always keep watching that the sandpaper does not cut through the glass covering. When the board appears finished take a long careful look all over to make sure the job is perfect and there are no shiny spots left. If you're satisfied with your work it's time for glossing.

The Gloss Coat

Before mixing up a batch of resin and catalyst be sure the work area is free from dust. Next, the board should be cleaned of all sand particles. A vacuum cleaner with a dust brush does a good job. After the initial dusting, wipe the board down with a clean rag dampened with acetone. This will pick up the remaining particles.

Now mix resin and catalyst. Mix enough to cover both sides at the same time; about one and one-half quarts. The gloss coat requires a finishing resin. This type of resin has a finishing agent added to improve its flowing qualities. Before applying the finishing resin, place masking tape around the edges. The tape should be laid on about one-half inch below the center line of the rail. This allows an overlap of resin on the rails and an even lap line.

When the resin and catalyst are mixed the resin is poured on slowly. Then, with a pure bristle brush, smooth the resin on carefully, attempting to achieve an even coat. Some of the resin will drip off, which is normal. As soon as the dripping has stopped and the resin has jelled, pull off the tape. When the resin has set and become hard, sand down the ridge left where the tape and resin met. Now turn the board over and repeat the same steps on the other side.

The Color Coat

If a color coat is desired the procedure is somewhat different. For color, obtain a special resin pigment. Follow the manufacturer's instructions for mixing with resin. Too much color pigment will slow the drying time of the resin. After the pigment is mixed with the resin, strain the liquid through clean cheesecloth or paint filters. Sometimes the pigment will not completely dissolve and the little particles should be filtered out to prevent them from becoming part of the color coat.

Again tape the edges. Use a bristle brush for spreading the resin and proceed as above. If a colored design or stripes are desired, mask off the area to be pigmented with masking tape. Brush on resin and pigment smoothly. As soon as the resin has been applied, pull off the tape. This allows the resin to spread slightly and results in a smooth edge between the colored area and the noncolored surface.

Sometimes after the color has been applied, another coat of clear resin can be applied for added gloss and beauty. When applying the clear coat be sure to use a brush that is absolutely clear, or better yet a new brush. The slightest trace of colored resin will taint the clear resin.

High Gloss Polish

For a new-car-type high gloss the freshly fiberglassed board can be given a polish. Sometimes streaks appear in the finishing resin. This is caused by the substance added to improve the flow quality. These streaks and other minor flaws or small particles of dust and dirt can be removed by polishing. First, remove any particles or imperfections with fine wet-or-dry sandpaper. Then take powdered pumice paste and polish lightly, either by hand or with an electric polisher. It may take two or more pumice applications to eliminate all traces of particles. For the final polish use a rubbing compound such as the red Simonize auto type. For the high gloss, buff with a high-grade auto paste wax.

Your board is now ready for the surf, but don't forget that after all this work is done there's still one job left—the paraffin rubdown on the top deck.

Chapter 16

BOARD CARE AND REPAIR

MOST people regard their boards with pride and attempt to keep them in good condition. Like any piece of sports equipment that takes hard knocks, a surfboard, though amazingly tough, is bound to be damaged at one time or another. The main cause of dings, or damaged areas, is strong impact on sharp objects. The fiberglass covering on a board is brittle. Even three and four layers of glass cloth can't overcome the inherent brittleness of the glass-resin lamination. A board can fly through the air, land on the sand, and absorb the shock without a trace of damage because the shock is spread over a wide area. But a collision against a sharp rock, or another board, will punch a hole through even the toughest fiberglass covering. A board landing on its tail, rail, or nose will suffer considerable damage. Most fractures, or dings, can be prevented by careful handling of the board during transit, keeping the board from washing in on rocks after a wipe-out, and avoiding collisions with other boards.

The current modern foam and fiberglass board is relatively non-moisture-absorbent. Water will enter a puncture, but it won't spread far under the covering unless the hole is large. Still, in time, the foam will become discolored, and rot will start the process of deterioration. It's best to fix dings as soon as possible. Minor repairs—scratches on the board's surface or small hairline cracks—do not require immediate attention, but if a good chunk of the nose or tail is ripped off, better call a halt to surfing and get the damage repaired. Loose fiberglass edges are a hazard to both the surfer and those riding next to him. A torn, jagged piece of glass cuts deep and leaves a nasty laceration. If there's a flap of glass hanging loose from the nose of your board, and you're getting dirty looks from people around you, you'll know why.

In prolonged exposure to hot sun and excessive dampness, the glass tends to discolor slightly if it is the normal neutral shade. Hot sun will also cause moisture trapped under the glass skin to expand. If the expansion occurs where the pressure can't be released through cracks or holes, the cloth rises from the foam and a blister results. Better to store boards out of the direct rays of the sun.

Boards kept in an excessively damp place absorb moisture if there are any cracks in the surface of the glass. A good general rule: treat a board like a good piece of furniture—excessive dampness and heat are to be avoided.

Repairing a Ding

Injuries to boards fall into two categories. The minor ding requires only filling the hole and recovering. The major ding requires extensive repair, such as cutting out the damaged area, replacing with new foam and recovering. The following example demonstrates how both processes of repair were combined to fix a break.

Before starting to work with fiberglass and resin, gather all the materials. Running out of resin or catalyst in the middle of a job is annoying. Many hardware stores and hobby shops sell fiberglass repair kits that contain the necessary materials for small jobs. If there are many dings to repair, plus other jobs calling for fiberglass, buy larger amounts of materials. If you've built a board recently, the leftover glass and resin (if it's fresh) may suffice. Below is a list of necessary materials for fixing a ding:

—Fiberglass cloth, enough for the job and if possible the same weight and weave as the original.

—Laminating resin, for the first coat—a pint.

—Gloss coat resin—a pint.

—Catalyst—enough for the job and a little extra; follow instructions on container for mixing.

—Sandpaper, quantities of it. Coarse open coat for the rough sanding, medium open coat for the last sanding.

—Acetone—to clean brushes and whatever is spilled on the garage floor.

—Paintbrush, two- or three-inch. Since resin will dissolve the paint on the handle and the color will get in the gloss coat, be careful, or use a brush with no color.

—Clean containers for mixing resin and catalyst. Paper cups will do.

—Thickener, to be added to the resin to make a filler paste to pack in the damaged area.

Fixing a ding is a little like being a fiberglass dentist, except the cavity is in the board. If the glass is merely cracked and there is no damaged area underneath, a patch may be applied directly over the crack. Before starting, remove any wax from the general area. The wax can be cleaned off with acetone and sandpaper. Don't use oil-base paint thinners for cleaning, or in any phase of the fiberglassing process; they are not compatible with polyester resins.

Place the board in the sun for a few days for the damaged area to dry out. Remove the broken and crushed fiberglass. Cut out a wedge slightly larger than the damaged area. Make the edges of the cut quite sharp to permit a precise fitting of the new wedge. From a scrap piece of foam, shape a wedge that will fit exactly into the cut. Cut the new fiberglass cloth to make a patch over the area. The patch should overlap the area being repaired by an inch or more. Since the ding is on the rail, place the board on its side and tape newspapers below to prevent resin from dripping on the undamaged sides. Mix half a cup of resin with catalyst, fol-

1. The torn fiberglass and crushed foam are removed prior to inserting a filler wedge. The area where the new fiberglass will be applied is cleaned of wax and dirt.

2. Foam wedge has been inserted. Polyester resin has been used as glue to fix the wedge to the foam. Next the wedge will be trimmed flush to rail of board.

3. The fiberglass and resin have been applied to the patch area. The masking tape was pulled. After the resin has set, the loose strands of fiberglass will be sanded off and a gloss coat of resin brushed on. Board will then be ready to surf again.

lowing the manufacturer's directions. Conduct these repairs in a shaded area to prevent the resin from hardening too quickly. Resin must be used as soon as it is activated with catalyst. Coat the wedge and the cut with the liquid and insert the wedge. The resin serves as glue to hold and fix the wedge into the cut. Within fifteen minutes the resin hardens and the wedge is firmly in place. Next, the portions of the wedge protruding beyond the rail are sanded flush with the rail. The sanding brings the foam wedge down to the exact circumference of the rail and also cleans the area to help the new resin adhere to the old glass.

Tape the fiberglass patch to the rail. Take care to make the glass cloth fit smoothly. (The tape creates a dam, preventing the resin from working over to other areas.) With a clean paintbrush, apply the resin to the cloth. *Saturate the cloth completely and smooth out bubbles that form under the cloth.* As soon as the resin jells, lift the tape off (after the resin hardens, the tape may be impossible to remove). The time from the jelled state to the completely cured and hardened state is an hour or so, depending on amount of catalyst, temperature, and sunlight. After the laminating resin has hardened, smooth over any rough edges with sandpaper.

The gloss coat, if carefully applied, almost completely hides the repaired area. Before glossing, give the whole area a light going over with medium grit sandpaper; this roughens the surface slightly and makes for better adhesion when the gloss is applied. Clean the area with acetone, which picks up dust and sanded fiberglass particles. Apply masking tape around the area to be glossed. Apply the glossing resin with a clean natural bristle brush. As soon as the resin is applied, pull the tape. This lets the resin flow slightly and makes for a smoother edge. The patch should now be indistinguishable. If flaws or roughness appear they can be removed by polishing. To polish, rub lightly with very fine wet-or-dry sandpaper. Next polish again with automobile rubbing compound, giving the area plenty of hard buffing. For high gloss, use auto wax and more buffing.

And last—place brushes in acetone as quickly as possible after they have been in resin. A resin-wet two-dollar brush allowed to sit for even five minutes will be ruined.

Minor Repairs

If very small dings and slight punctures occur they can be sealed quickly with a drop or two of resin. Make sure the area around the hole is clean and buffed slightly with sandpaper. If a small puncture occurs while surfing it can be plugged by rubbing wax in the hole. This will keep the water out until repair can be made. If the nose, tail, or rail is fractured, black plastic electricians' tape can be used to cover the ding temporarily. Some very serious surfers keep fiberglass repair kits in their cars and fix dings on the spot. Small slits in the top or bottom can be repaired by laying a strip of glass over the cut area and applying resin. Unless the damaged area is compressed and torn it need not be cut out.

GLOSSARY

ANGLING—Sliding across the face of a wave, either right or left.

BACKWASH—The rush of water down the slope of the beach after a wave has run up the beach.

BAGGIES—Much too large swim trunks, worn as a fad by younger surfers.

BAILING OUT—A planned escape from the surfboard, just before the surfer would be wiped out.

BALSA WOOD—A soft, light, porous wood from South America, used for surfboards before foam and fiberglass.

BELLYBOARD—A short surfboard propelled mainly by swimfins. Called a PIAPO in Hawaii.

BIG GUN—An eleven-foot or longer surfboard specially designed for large waves.

BLOWN OUT—A surfing word with two meanings: (1) surf that has been wind-whipped sufficiently to make it unridable, (2) what happens when offshore winds blow a surfer off the top of a wave and down the back side.

BOMBOARA—An Australian word that refers to a big wave that breaks outside the normal surf line.

BOTTOM TURN—A swinging turn made at the bottom or well below the crest of a wave.

BOWL—The rising of a wave caused by rolling over a shallow portion of the bottom. The rising of the bottom causes the wave to break somewhat harder and faster.

CATALYST—The agent which causes the resin used in surfboard building to harden.

CHANNEL—A spot of deep water where the surf doesn't usually form; a good place to paddle out.

CHOPPY—A ruffled water surface caused by winds. A sea state prior to the formation of whitecaps.

CLIMBING—Angling up the face of a wave toward the crest.

CLOSE-OUT—A wave or series of waves that curls over all at once and can't be ridden, or when the waves become too big to ride.

CREST—The top portion of a wave. When a wave is cresting it is just beginning to spill over and break.

CURL—The portion of the wave that is spilling over and breaking. SHOOTING THE CURL is riding the wave right where it is breaking and forming a tube or tunnel.

CUT BACK—To turn toward the breaking part of the wave.

CUT OUT—To pull out of the wave, like kicking out.

DECK—The top surface of the surfboard.

DING—A hole in or injury to the surface of the surfboard.

DROP—The first downward slide made during the start.

DROP IN—A big surf term meaning to continue the slide down the face of the wave to gain speed.

DUMPED—A body surfing term meaning to get tossed down by a wave.

FACE—The unbroken front of the wave.

FIBERGLASS—Glass cloth used in surfboard construction.

FIN—A skeg (see Skeg).

FINS—Swim fins or flippers used in body surfing or skin diving, worn on the feet to increase the effectiveness of the kick.

GLASS-OFF—When the surf becomes smooth after the wind dies.

GLASSY—A smooth water surface condition caused by absence of local winds.

GOOFY-FOOT—A surfer who rides with his right foot forward. (Left foot forward is the normal stance.)

GRABBING THE RAIL—A pullout technique done by grabbing the rail on the side away from the wave and pulling the board into the wave to keep it from being washed away; used by some surfers to steady themselves while riding in the curl or tube.

GREMLIN—A young surfer, sometimes a rowdy, who is just beginning. (Not a flattering term.)

HANGING FIVE (or ten)—Placing the toes over the nose or extreme forward portion of the board.

HEAD DIP—A forward riding style where the head is lowered almost to the nose of the board.

HEAVIES—Big surf.

HOOK—The curling portion of a wave.

HOT-DOGGING—Fancy surfing done by a skilled surfer.

HUMPING—Waves rising up suddenly just before breaking, used sometimes to refer to big waves.

INSHORE—The place in the water just off the beach and inside the break.

INSIDE—The surfing area nearest the beach.

KELP—Seaweed that floats on the surface though the roots are anchored to the bottom.

KICK OUT—Pushing down on the tail of the board to lift and turn the nose over the top of the wave.

LEFT SLIDE—Riding a wave to the surfer's left.

LOCKED IN—Firmly set in the curling portion of the wave with water holding down the tail of the board.

LINES—A series of waves rolling in with some consistency.

OUTSIDE—The area beyond where the surf is breaking. Also the yell or warning which means a wave is coming.

OVER THE FALLS—Driven down with the breaking part of the wave, toward the bottom, with force.

PADDLEBOARD—A hollow wooden (or very light foam) elongated surfboard used primarily to travel across the water. Most paddleboards are awkward in the surf.

PAIPO BOARD—The Hawaiian term for bellyboard, a short surfboard.

PEAK—The highest part of the wave.

PEARL—A surfboard "pearls" when the nose drops enough to dig in and slow or stop the board.

PIER BREAK—Waves that break next to or under a pier, sometimes used when a pier actually starts a wave breaking.

PIG BOARD—A surfboard with a pointed nose and a broad tail.

PIN TAIL—A surfboard with a long tapering stern which comes almost to a point.

POLYURETHANE—The most common type of foam used in surfboard construction.

POP-OUTS—Mass-produced surfboards of low quality.

POUNDERS—Crashing, unridable waves.

PULL OUT—Ending the ride and getting off the wave by steering the board over, or through, the face of the wave.

QUASIMODO—Riding forward in a hunched-over position; named after the Hunchback of Notre Dame.

RAILS—The rounded edges of the surfboard.

REEF—Rock, coral, or sand which lies below the surface causing incoming swells to shoal and break.

RESIN—The liquid plastic used to laminate glass cloth to foam in surfboard construction.

RIGHT SLIDE—Riding a wave to the surfer's right.

RIP CURRENT (or tide)—A volume of water moving seaward or parallel to shore caused by massive amounts of water piling up alongshore and then moving out seeking equilibrium.

ROCKER—The concave lengthwise curve in a surfboard.

SET—A group of waves.

SHOOTING THE TUBE OR CURL—Riding through, or in and out of the hollow part of the wave formed as it crests over.

SHOREBREAK—Waves that break on shore with considerable energy. Surf not breaking well for riding.

SHOULDER—The unbroken portion of the wave next to the white water.

SHUFFLE—A movement toward the nose of the board done by moving one foot after another and not crossing the feet.

SKEG—The fin at the tail of the board.

SLIDING—Riding down the wave after catching it.

SOUP—The foamy part of the broken wave, the white water.

SPILLER—A wave that begins cresting at the top and breaks gradually forward.

SPINNER—A complete 360-degree turn made by the standing surfer while his board keeps going straight.

STALL—Slowing the board after it outraces the wave, so that the break can catch up with the surfer.

STRINGER—The wood strip running down the center of the board. Used for strength and to set the rocker. Sometimes used for design.

SURFARI—A surfing trip, a hunt for good surf.

SWELLS—Unbroken waves moving in groups of similar height and period. Their form is like that of a sine curve.

TAIL—The stern or rear end of the surfboard.

TAKEOFF—The start of a ride.

TANDEM—Two people on one board, most often a man and woman.

TRIM—To steer the board so it planes most efficiently across the face of a wave. A board in trim should be moving at maximum speed and stability.

TROUGH—The lowest part between the crests of two waves.

TUBE—The hollow portion of a wave formed when the crest spills over and makes a tunnel or hollow space in front of the face of the wave.

UNDERTOW—There is no such thing. What is thought to be "undertow" is really a backwash of water running down the slope of a steep beach.

UNITED STATES SURFING ASSOCIATION (USSA)—An organization of surfers formed for the betterment of the sport.

WALKING THE NOSE—Moving forward on the board toward the front or nose.

WALL—The face of a wave, usually steep, unbroken.

WET SUIT—A neoprene rubber suit used by skin divers and surfers to keep warm. A wet suit allows water to enter between the rubber and the skin. The water is then trapped and the body warms it.

WHITECAPS—Waves or swells, usually at sea, the tops blown off by the wind, forming white spume.

WHITE WATER—The white bubbly, foamy part of a broken wave. Also called soup.

WIPE-OUT—Falling or being knocked, blown, or pushed off a board by a collapsing wave.

WOODY—A wooden-bodied station wagon.

INDEX

217